PRAISE FOR

Lead from Your Heart

"This highly practical and beautifully written book affirms my belief that our most valuable currency is relationship and that the conversation is the relationship. Better yet, it shows us how to have those conversations, providing real life examples about issues all of us can relate to. As a bonus, if you want to learn how to move from WTF to SWN, you'll have to read it to find out. It will be worth it."

– *Susan Scott, author of* Fierce Conversations, Achieving Success at Work & in Life – One Conversation at a Time

"As we move into the fullness of the 21st century, how we relate to each other is the imperative of our time. This book is a testimony to the power of collaborative partnership and clear directive on the vital importance of finding our way through and beyond what divides us. In *Lead from Your Heart: The Art of Relationship-based Leadership,* authors Tanya Schecter and Matthew Gould offer an accessible and yet profound model that shows us how to strengthen our relationships by understanding how to embrace conflict, disagree creatively and lead from our hearts… together."

– *Karen and Henry Kimsey-House, Co-Founders, The Co-Active™ Training Institute*

"Insightful and engaging! *Lead from Your Heart* is the ultimate guide to empathetic leadership. Tanya and Matthew show how relationships and trust are the true center of good leadership that will help you lead better and achieve more than ever before."

– *Marshall Goldsmith, New York Times #1 bestselling author of* Triggers, Mojo, *and* What Got You Here Won't Get You There, *and* Thinkers 50 #1 *Executive Coach and only two-time #1 Leadership Thinker in the world.*

"This is a book for anyone who cares about their relationships. It is clear and concisely written with excellent strategies for addressing conflict and deepening connections. An excellent tool for managers, relationship therapists, parents and couples."

– *Dr. Marilee Sigal, PsyD RCC, Relationship & Sex Therapist*

"I ate this book up! It's an absolute must-read for those who want to foster value-driven relationships both personally and professionally. Tanya and Matt have created a powerful and practical roadmap for living our values and fostering authentic and loving connections with those around us... *Lead from Your Heart* provides clear and actionable steps for building relationships that are positive, awake, and forward moving... I'm so grateful they have brought this to the world!"

– *Rachel Scott, MSci & MFA, Consultant, Educator, and author of* Head over Heels: A Yogi's Guide to Dating

"Meaningful relationships are THE foundation of successful businesses... we wouldn't be half the business we are today if we hadn't learned how to strengthen relationships, navigate conflict and build trust. *Lead from Your Heart* is THE book to read if you want to build your skills in these areas!"

– *Brian Scudamore, Founder & CEO, O2E Brands & 1-800-GOT-JUNK?*

"In my work with executives, conflict and relationships are consistent areas of focus for our development and coaching conversations. There are a host of assessments that help identify styles and diagnose the situation. There are fewer resources that provide guidance on "how" to improve the relationship and engage conflict to deepen it. *Lead from Your Heart* goes beyond other books by providing a map and a set of practical tools to build and deepen relationships that are needed, not just to get results but to unlock the potential and passion of employees, peers, and partners. It's worth the time to read and, even more important, the investment of time to apply. You will be a better leader, colleague, and partner because of it!"

– Karen Mathre, PCC, Director, Leadership and Coaching Multinational Medical Technology Company

"The greatest gift *Lead from Your Heart* gives us is the invitation to take responsibility for ourselves and our relationships in service of creating positive change. Tanya and Matthew skillfully share real-life examples that read like a novel, while cementing the universal truth about relationships – that we are all interconnected and interdependent. This book is easy to navigate, with tools, key take-aways, and practical applications that anyone can use to start transforming their relationships today."

– Alia Allison, CPCC, Director, Talent Development, Gap Inc.

"*Lead from Your Heart* masterfully slays the myth that leadership is a solo mission. Packed with insights and useful techniques, Tanya Schecter and Matthew Gould provide a wonderful playbook to get you leading through your relationships, grounded by values and enacted by key responsibilities."

– Dan Pontefract, Leadership Strategist and author of LEAD. CARE. WIN.

"In a world that has gone more-than-slightly mad, *Lead from Your Heart* is a powerful call back to center. To a center where we are not alone, and from which we can always lead: the fluid and ever-changing waters of relationship. The solutions to today's problems will come from those who can create from and through our connection, and this is the way that Tanya and Matthew point to with their inspired leadership model. Timeless and forward-looking, *Lead from Your Heart* is a path to a future where we *all* belong."

– Molly Flanagan, PCC, CPCC, ORSCC, Capacity Development Officer, United Nations Department of Operational Support

"If we want to succeed in life and in business, we need to build strong relationships, have compassion for others and communicate effectively. Yet at some point, for all of us, even our best relationships can be challenging. *Lead from Your Heart* provides a powerful roadmap and thoughtful tools you can implement immediately to enhance both your personal and professional relationships. I encourage everyone to read this insightful book and put into practice the solution-based approach that Tanya and Matthew have created."

– Stephanie Colegrove, MBA, CPCU, CPCC, ACC, Executive Coach and Speaker, former Operations Vice President, State Farm Insurance

"As humans, organizations, and systems interact on a global scale, our world is calling for a more generous way of being together. We must shift from being certain and right about ourselves to being curious and open with each other. *Lead from Your Heart* provides a framework and language that helps us improve and leverage the most powerful resource we have as humans — our relationships."

– Trina Hamilton, M.Ed., CPCC, ACC, Executive Coach, former Head of Leadership Development, Coast Capital Savings

"I have always said, 'Don't promote people to leadership positions unless they sincerely like people!' Salaries and bonuses don't motivate engagement. People give their best efforts and generate important ideas when they feel safe and cared about by their leaders, especially in difficult times when emotions are high. *Lead from Your Heart* maps out what leaders must do to connect both with themselves and others to create the meaningful connections that inspire great work. It should become a classic guide to follow world-wide."

– Marcia Reynolds, PsyD, past global chair of the International Coach Federation and author of Coach the Person, Not the Problem: A User's Guide to Reflective Inquiry

"Do you ever wish that you had a way to navigate conflict more effectively? Well, here's your guide. Drawing on Co-Active Leadership principles and ideas from Brene Brown, John Gottman and others, Tanya Schecter and Matthew Gould have created a beautiful model, guide and process for learning how to create empowered relationships and true leadership with heart, smarts and clarity."

– Cynthia Loy Darst, MFA, MCC ORSCC, author of Meet Your Inside Team: How To Turn Internal Conflict Into Clarity and Move Forward With Your Life

"Whether you're leading a movement, a family or a business *Lead from Your Heart* will give you the roadmap you need to get where you're going, as your truest, purest, highest self. You'll get what's needed for relationship health, and the essential tools to deepen your practices. Matt and Tanya courageously share the words of their very own hearts for the sake of our collective relationships."

– Kasey Matz, MA, ACC, ORSCC, CDWF, Leadership Coach and Project Director, University of Colorado

"In business, as in life, we get things done with and through other people. In our mad rush for efficiency and effectiveness, we sometimes forget that the quality of our relationships largely determines our success or failure. *Lead from Your Heart* offers a doorway into being in relationship with one another – and ourselves – with a powerful map that leads us back to connection and meaningful collaboration when our relationships go sideways. It provides actionable ways to practice being in relationship, first with ourselves and what is most important to us, then with others as we become more conscious of our impact on and with others. Using the HTI Relationship Map, Tanya and Matt take us on a journey of leadership from the inside out, and illustrate it with real-world examples that demonstrate its effectiveness. *Lead from Your Heart* is foundational must-read for leaders ready to take full responsibility for their world and their connection to others."

– Carlo Delumpa, CPCC, Leadership and Executive Coach, and faculty member for the Co-Active Training Institute

LEAD

FROM YOUR HEART

The Art of
Relationship-based
Leadership

Tanya Schecter and Matthew Gould

HTI
INSTITUTE

Editor: Greg Ioannou
Front cover design: Sean Strong and Howard VanEs
Interior graphics: @ 2020 HTI Institute Inc.

ISBNs: 978-1-7771036-0-6 (paperback), 978-1-77180-410-3 (epub),
978-1-77180-411-0 (Kindle).

This is the original print edition of *Lead from Your Heart: The
Art of Relationship-based Leadership*.

Table of Contents

To Olivier and Josh, you have my heart.
Now and forever. – Tanya

To Susie, Megan, Sarah, and Charlie
and my extended family. – Matt

We're all hungry for connection, intimacy, and deep, meaningful relationships.

INTRODUCTION

Hearts Together Inspire

It was the most toxic work environment I've ever experienced. I was working as a consultant in a large regional government organization. Despite having a mandate of employee health and wellness, employees routinely walked through the door with their heads down, surreptitiously checking the clock to note their daily start times as they slunk into their cubicles and inserted a set of earphones, hoping to avoid all human contact. It was unionized, and most employees were lifers, only working the requisite number of hours while hanging on to the prospect of their next vacation like a temporary lifeboat as they counted down the days until their retirement. Misery abounded.

From managers on down, tension seeped throughout the atmosphere. Distrust ran rampant and business decisions were based on what could entrench personal power positions, regardless of organizational and project needs. The result was an environment in which permanent employees feared sharing their expertise. They worked at a lower level than they were capable of and often became sick or took stress leave. Consultants left as soon as they realized their expertise was unwelcome and they'd never be effective, blocked by managers who feared losing their power.

I realized I was seeing unhappiness, detachment, and toxicity caused by leaders who:

+ chose the bottom line over relationships;
+ were driven by fear or ego, reluctant to ask for help or admit to making mistakes;
+ used a model of "you're for me or against me," requiring people to take sides and adopt positions based on absolute beliefs;
+ did whatever they wanted, treating people without regard for their feelings, a practice bolstered by their belief that questioning their decisions or perspective meant you were disloyal.

There was a widespread belief that only those granted specific job titles can lead, make decisions, or have an impact. The result was a group of humans sitting next to one another daily who were lonely, disconnected, disempowered, ineffective, and unhappy. They distrusted each other and operated without purpose or fulfillment.

I observed this pattern in various work environments for many years before I began to understand what I was seeing and piece together a solution. What I was seeing included:

+ relationships are perceived as expendable and a luxury rather than an essential requirement for growth and achievement to occur;
+ our relationships are often superficial and fraught with tension;
+ unresolved conflicts abound;

- important conversations are avoided;
- technology has overtaken our lives and impacts how we interact;
- people are feeling various levels of disconnection;
- toxicity affects our health, our productivity, and our ability to effect outcomes we desire;
- our results are less than what they could be, and our values are widely professed but not always lived.

Ultimately, we've largely lost the ability to communicate in a rich and meaningful way that yields positive results even though we, individually and as a society, have a hunger for richer and stronger relationships, intimacy, authenticity, and deep connection. We want our lives to have meaning and we want to be impactful and fulfilled. These inabilities limit our ability to be effective leaders.

As soon as I realized that we're all searching for this intimacy and connection, it dawned on me that I'd never be able to find a solution to broken relationships on my own. It was in my search to reach out to others that the HTI (Hearts Together Inspire) Relationship Map was born. It's a great map. Of course, I didn't create it alone. It's a map created through my relationship and partnership with Matt.

Matt and I met at a ten-month Co-Active™ Leadership program. I had come to the program with twenty plus years of experience running my business and acting as a performance consultant and coach. During this time, I'd worked in a variety of industries and organizations with people at all levels, completing countless projects while navigating change. Although I had many repeat clients and often hired and worked with the same consultants, I largely ran my business on my own. After two decades of being the only person in the driver's seat, I was tired of it. The advantages of being in this position no longer outweighed the limitations I was brushing up against. I was at the Leadership program hoping to find someone I could partner with: someone with whom I could develop a trusted relationship and who I could count on to push me to play to my edges, challenge me to set higher goals that fall in line with my values, and co-create on an intellectual level. I was tired of working by myself and wanted to form a "we."

Conversely, Matt was a one-man band and liked it that way. He'd worked as an employee at a large telecommunications company for over a decade, rising through the ranks up to a directorship position where he focused on leadership. Since leaving, he'd built up his sole proprietorship and developed leadership academies while focusing on working with companies that wanted to increase their leadership capabilities and capacities. Matt came to the Leadership program looking to expand his business, not build personal relationships. From the beginning, we were like oil and water.

Matt and I first met on the morning of the first of four week-long Co-Active™ Leadership retreats. After barely making eye contact or asking me my name, he sipped his coffee and started grilling me on what I did for a living, who my clients were, and what my annual net revenue was. I thought he was a total jerk. This perception was reinforced throughout the week as I noticed him glad-handing his way through the other twenty-two people in our group, wanting to win each of them over to his fan base.

Yet, as the week went by, I noticed a few other things about him. He was noticeably nervous when he had to climb to great heights and was willing to admit his fear and ask for help. He allowed tears, arising from an overflowing heart, to slide down an unabashedly open face and consistently attempted to step out of his comfort zone by trying on new behaviors. All of this made me think that perhaps there was more to him than what first met my eye. By the end of the week, my interest was piqued.

I began noticing Tanya during the first retreat when our group was in the middle of typing each person according to how we naturally present ourselves and show up in the world. Although everyone else gracefully and willingly accepted their type and the overarching label that categorized them, Tanya wasn't having it. From my perspective, her lack of willingness to accept how we were typing her was creating unnecessary friction and slowing the group down. It was making me uncomfortable and I wished she'd just accept her type, let it go, and realize it wasn't a big deal. As my frustration mounted, I could feel my eyes roll into the back of my head as negative and judgmental thoughts quickly followed.

As the week passed, though, I noticed that while Tanya didn't create unnecessary conflict, she was willing to take a stand when she felt something was out of alignment or integrity, regardless of the conflict this created. I also noticed she was willing to stay in the conflict and with the other person until the issue was resolved. All of this was outside of my comfort zone. It occurred to me that to truly step into my leadership and develop my capabilities, I was going to have to get comfortable with conflict and Tanya might be the perfect person to do this with.

At the end of the week, Matt and I said goodbye to one another at the retreat center. Two hours later, we found ourselves face-to-face at the airport as we discovered we were destined for the same flight home. Talking together, our defenses started to break down. Although we were meant to be sitting in different rows, the person sitting next to Matt offered to switch seats with me, noting we were clearly enjoying each other and our conversation.

Over the next three hours, Matt and I touched on a range of subjects – our thoughts and feelings about what we'd experienced over the past week, our initial perceptions, assumptions, and judgments about each other, and the visions, aspirations, and desires we had for ourselves as leaders moving forward. By the end of our trip, we decided we might like to work together and that we'd partner on the project recently assigned to us at our leadership program, using it as a testing ground to see how we functioned together.

While it would have been ideal if we'd moved smoothly into partnership with one another, our relationship's beginning was bumpy. It took us a great many conversations to work through areas of conflict and our differing approaches to conflict before we could truly work together and form a partnership founded on trust, intimacy, and connection. This still takes effort.

The HTI Relationship Map was born out of the process of creating our partnership. We developed it to help guide our relationship to a deeper level where we could both live within our values, take responsibility, own our impacts, and develop our relationship through honest connection and conversation, even when differences appeared. As we realized its universal applicability, it became one of our guiding passions to discover how, together, we could use it to make a positive impact on the world. The Map allows all of us to stay in relationships as we navigate conflict together, and emerge from conflict as a stronger unit that can create the world we want to live in.

The HTI Relationship Map is a model that brings our relationships – our relationship with ourself[1] and our

---

1. While not grammatically correct, we are using the word ourself, instead of ourselves, to refer to our individual personhood and sense of self, essentially what composes our inner identity.

relationship with others (friends, family, community, teams, businesses, organizations) – back to the forefront of our interactions. This focus on relationships better equips us to connect with one another, be accountable for our impact, live on purpose and in alignment with our values, accomplish our goals, and be the leaders we're destined to be. The HTI Relationship Map offers us a way to bypass the superficial as we navigate real conflict and emergent issues, so we can come out stronger on the other side, together.

How Should I Approach This Book?

Although the HTI Relationship Map is based on multiple concepts that can be used on their own or in combination with others, this book is designed to be read in the sequence provided. Each chapter covers one HTI Relationship Map concept that you can use immediately, on its own, or in tandem with any of the ones already covered. Tips and exercises to help you apply each concept are included at each chapter's end.

Chapter One looks at why relationships matter, what it means to be a leader, why navigating conflict is imperative to the success of our relationships, and how the HTI Relationship Map can help us navigate conflict and strengthen our relationships. Chapter Two explores the concept of full responsibility, for ourselves and for the impact our relationships have on the outer world. Chapter Three covers the meaning and use of personal and relationship values.

Chapter Four delves in the concept of stay: staying in conflict and discomfort, staying with our and others' emotions, staying in integrity with our values, and staying in relationship with one another as we navigate these together. Chapter Five explains what a relationship stake is and how to create and use one for maximum impact.

The concepts covered in the first five chapters help us identify where we are in the present moment: in a relationship or not, hearts together, touching, or apart. They increase our awareness and yet, without additional tools, don't help us navigate towards our desired destination.

Chapters Six and Seven explain heart-centered tools that help us navigate to a new and preferred destination. Chapter Six provides a description of STCI (Stop, Think, Choose, Implement) and how we can use it as a navigational system when change (positive or negative) occurs. Chapter Seven explains the four HTI Relationship Cornerstones and how we can apply them to achieve greater intimacy and improved outcomes when we experience conflict.

The final chapter, Chapter Eight, explores the concept of "So, What Now?" and how we can apply it to keep ourselves in alignment as we travel from where we were, to where we are, to where we want to go... together. This chapter looks at how, together, we can accomplish so much and how, also together, we are better.

Note to the Reader from Tanya and Matt

As appropriate, our personal stories of our learned approaches to relationships and conflict, including our relationship with each other, are included to illustrate HTI Relationship Map concepts and ideas. While the stories we've included are personal, they represent universal issues impacting all interactions and relationships, issues that often limit their potential and eventual success. This is as true for families and friends as it is for colleagues, teams, managers, employees, and leaders at all levels.

This book is primarily written in Tanya's voice to create a continuous narrative that's easy to read. Matt's stories are presented in italics and are told from his perspective. Regardless of voice, the content in this book represents both of our ideas, thoughts, and perspectives. It's the result of a true collaboration, one we hope will enrich your life and relationships.

The quality of our relationships impacts how we feel, physically and emotionally, and our overall sense of well-being.

CHAPTER ONE

Relationships Matter

We're all unique. From our heads down to our toes and all throughout our souls, each of us is a distinct being. What we think about, how we think, what we care about, how we show compassion, and the actions and behaviors we take vary from person to person and from situation to situation. In addition to our uniqueness, every moment we experience is different and constantly in a state of flux. Shifting sands form a dynamic and often unpredictable footing beneath us, making it difficult to stand, let alone move forward. This dynamic is even more tricky when we're in a relationship with another person, trying to move forward together, since we may or may not share the same underlying beliefs, values, perspectives, interpretations, hopes, desires, and goals.

Although they take work and it may be tempting to avoid them, relationships matter. They're a fundamental aspect of what makes us human. Relationships provide us with connection, purpose, a sense of belonging, and a place where we can be seen, heard, appreciated, and affirmed. In our relationships, we find our significance. They're the source of knowing we matter.

Our relationships can also provide us with a sense of safety. When we feel safe in our relationships, we can be vulnerable, drop our emotional armor, and reveal our cracks, knowing we will be cared for regardless. Through relationships, we experience intimacy, trust, and love. We not only survive but become stronger and more powerful, maximizing our own potential and that of our relationships. When positive, our relationships nurture us, and we're better able to grow and create. We're also able to lean into one another so our sum becomes greater than our individual parts. More becomes possible.

Ultimately, the quality of our relationships determines how we feel, physically and emotionally, and our overall sense of well-being. Bad relationships can be toxic, leading to ill-health, disconnection, and unhappiness, whereas good relationships are generative, inspiring, expansive, nurturing, and connective. All these impacts have very real consequences for our quality of life.

What Do Relationships Have to Do with Leadership?

I'd taken the leap! After eleven years at an established corporation and a successful run up the ladder to director level, I found myself at a risky start up. With funding in place, an aggressive growth strategy, and a small team in hand, we embarked on establishing a brand-new wireless network and sales and distribution channels in a race to sign up mobile subscribers and exceed our investors' expectations. As the General Manager for Western Canada, I was responsible for building and leading a significantly important team and territory.

Nine months into the new role, I was failing. We weren't opening retail partners fast enough and many of the stores we'd opened weren't performing at projected levels. The positive relationship I'd initially formed with my boss was breaking apart as we felt mounting pressure. Trust between us further eroded as he began yelling and blaming my team and me for our lackluster results, and I placated him by telling him everything was ok, we just needed more time. Ten months in, results were no different and our relationship was extremely toxic. Then, my phone rang.

As I picked it up, I heard our company CFO's calm and trusted voice. "Hey Matt, it's Carl. I'm flying out tomorrow and I'd like to meet you in your office at 9:00 am."

"Awesome! I look forward to seeing you," I said confidently as my stomach turned and my knees shook. I was worried about my job, yet still looked forward to seeing Carl since I had a good relationship with him.

The next morning, Carl arrived on time, looked me in the eye, and asked, "How are you doing?"

"Great! It's so good to see you in our Western office," I said with a smile.

Carl paused and said, "No Matt, really, how are you doing?" With his hand on his briefcase, he said, "I have a really big check in here to make you and all the pressure go away. Is that what you want?"

In that moment, I realized I had a choice to lean into the mutual trust we'd built up in our relationship and open up to the cold hard truth, and told him "No, I definitely don't want that. And I need help."

"Let's get out of here and grab a coffee. I really want to understand where you're at."

Carl let me know that although he was sent out to fire me, he didn't agree with the decision. He'd always put human beings first and strongly believed that if he invested in a relationship, results would follow. He knew I was capable, despite recent results, and wanted to see if there was a possibility of following a different business strategy and achieving a different result with me staying in the general manager chair.

Over the next five hours, Carl's curiosity and genuine care for how I was approaching the business created an atmosphere in which we could have a powerful, truthful, and open conversation about my leadership, the strategy I was executing, our team's various elements, and our unique market conditions. Carl let me know which parts of my strategy he agreed with, offered feedback about parts he didn't, and invited me to look at new ideas and ways of organizing our team and focusing our efforts. The result was a fresh approach my team and I could begin executing immediately.

"I'm putting my neck on the line for you Matt, and I'm confident you and your team can pull it off," Carl said as he packed his bags, severance package tightly sealed inside. As he headed back to head office, he said, "The moment you need help, do me a favor, and just pick up the phone."

Carl's relationship-first approach made a difference. Slowly and surely, I began executing the plan we'd created together. Within six months, our results were improving. An open and truthful approach to reality also changed our office's culture. We immediately confronted issues, shifting our perspective and energy into seeing them as opportunities, while speaking the truth and working collaboratively with one another to resolve them. Seven months in, our new President praised my team for turning our performance around and exceeding most of our key metrics.

Carl's core belief in the power of relationships, his relationship with me, and the relationships I developed with my team and sales channel partners were instrumental in making this happen. The company saved money by not letting me go, stability resulted from low employee turnover, and our cultural shift towards trust and collaboration created a higher performing team. In this case, as always, relationships drove results.

We can't be effective leaders without being in relationships. Successful leaders foster great relationships with and among the people around them so they can lean into their relationships in times of misunderstanding, tension, and conflict and leverage them to create superior outcomes.

Relationships matter more than ever before. Governments, industries, and corporations are bending, violating, or outright breaking rules and laws at their convenience for the sake of profit and power. The internet and social media have created a layer of distance between us, all the while painting it with a false sense of intimacy. Our destination is uncertain, as are the various paths we can take to get there. We lack the navigational tools we need to move forward, in relationship and together.

Relationship-based leadership is key to improving personal fulfillment and happiness, employee engagement, customer experience, employee and customer churn, revenue, net profit, and environmental sustainability. It's also key to creating meaningful experiences within and between people so creativity, growth, and self-actualization can occur. All of these outcomes allow groups, teams, businesses, and us as humans to rise to the next levels of possibility.

I'm Not a Leader So Why Should I Care?

Many people think leadership comes from a job title, role, or function. We disagree. We believe leaders are people who have a vision and a purpose they feel compelled to take actions towards. They act in alignment with their values and live their lives on purpose, taking responsibility when they fall short. A leader is someone who finds their personal power and uses it to enrol others towards a vision. They don't give their power away based on how they're treated or because someone dismisses, ignores, or devalues them. A leader influences, creates, and raises up. Leaders inspire others.

Leaders foster and value their relationships, viewing them as sources of generative power they can tap into to achieve their vision and purpose. They remain grounded and centered when in the unknown, creating from others while letting go of the need to be the source of certainty. Their ability to let go of their own egos, while bringing others' talents and abilities to light, helps them create strong relationships. Within these relationships, beginning with the one they hold with themselves, they can tell the truth, engage in conflict, create positive outcomes, and emerge stronger, together.

Mahatma Gandhi is a great example of this definition of a leader. No matter how badly he was treated, dismissed, and mocked by the British Empire and her representatives, he never lost his sense of personal power or his ability to be impactful. Gandhi had a vision for his nation and fellow Indians of civil rights, peace, and freedom. As he traveled by foot across the nation to protest the British Salt Tax, he opened his heart to others while engaging in civil disobedience. Through these actions, he built personal relationships and unparalleled support for his vision and purpose. Eventually, because of his relationships and actions, the entire British Empire that had ruled the Indian subcontinent for centuries was brought to her knees.

While we can't be Gandhi, we can all be leaders. We are leaders when we consciously work to have an intended impact that's in alignment with our values and purpose, and when we take full responsibility if we fall short. We are leaders when we focus on developing our relationships, share responsibility for them, and show up authentically and vulnerably, daring to leave our egos at the door.

Each of us can choose to be and show up as a leader in our life, every day and in every interaction. Leadership is a choice and a set of actions. We believe our relationship with ourself is the best starting point for every leadership action. And, like any journey, we believe using a map helps us navigate more effectively.

What Do Maps Have to Do with Relationships and Leadership?

Maps help show us the way when we're lost. They're marked with clearly defined boundaries and specific labels (for example, London, Delhi, Vancouver, etc.) that allow us to quickly identify which map we should consult to pinpoint where we are in any given moment. Maps don't dictate where we must go or how we must get there. They simply provide us with reference points and navigational tools.

Maps provide us with choices when we want to get to a specific destination by showing us what's ahead and providing us with alternative routes. Without a map, it's harder for us to know if we've veered off course or unintentionally taken wrong turns that have hidden costs. Looking at a map also helps us stay together as we navigate our route side by side. It can also help us find one another if we drift apart or get lost. Finally, using a map provides us with unbiased guideposts that help us find our way and reduce our level of uncertainty and potential conflict as we navigate this process together.

When Matt and I began working together, conflicts continually arose. Through our conversations, we realized our perspectives and belief systems about conflict were very different. Digging deeper, it became apparent that, when it came to facing conflict together, we were starting from completely different locations, with very different guideposts. We'd each learned to deal with conflict using very different maps.

I come from a long line of tellers: people who know what should happen and what should be done. We come by it honestly. As Jews steeped in the Torah and the accompanying commentary spanning generations and centuries, we're taught practically right out of the womb that it's important to have an opinion and that it is critical to defend it. As Josh, my son, likes to joke, "Of course I have an opinion. At school, we're only twenty-four kids in our class but there are always thirty-five opinions. Debate is good and it feels great to be right." While having an opinion and being able to think critically have served me well, they've also come at a cost.

From a young age, I had big feelings and big emotions – and my parents taught me well to suppress or minimize them. When I was four, a witch visited *Sesame Street*, my favorite childhood show. I was so scared; I hid behind my mom's dresses and closed her closet door. When my mom asked me what I was doing in there, I shared my fears with her. She laughed, telling me not to be ridiculous and that what I had experienced wasn't real. She then went back to what she was doing. This set the stage for a lifetime of hiding and downplaying my feelings.

Then there was the day I was almost kidnapped in grade one. Having run home at breakneck speed to elude the predator at the end of our lane who was trying to lure me into her car, I burst into our house. Huffing and puffing, I breathed in terrified gasps, only to be met by my dad, who calmly looked up and dispassionately asked me, "What on earth took you so long?" As I blurted out what happened in a raspy voice, my dad rolled his eyes, and said, "Don't be ridiculous and stop exaggerating. Hurry up and eat your lunch or you'll be late getting back to school." Again, I was reminded that I shouldn't show fear or weakness.

As if that wasn't enough, one day when I was eleven, my dad took my brother and me out for lunch. As we sat down to eat, he said, "Your mother and I are getting divorced. We're going to sell the house and you'll both live with your mom in a new house we bought across town. In the meantime, I'm going to go to France with François, my boyfriend." I took this information in stride, in between bites of my baguette, as my dad continued. "You know what divorce means so it's not that big of a deal. Right?" "Right," I nodded, internally wondering what on earth it meant that my world was being turned upside down but knowing better, by now, than to share my feelings out loud.

This response pattern continued throughout my childhood, adolescence, and into adulthood. As I got older and my feelings became more complex, I learned that if I expressed them to my parents, I would be met with responses like "You're being unreasonable. Why do you think *that*? You're too anxious, just relax. That's not the way it is. You're making a big deal out of nothing. You're too demanding. What you should feel is…" Over time, I became very good at being self-sufficient, keeping my feelings and vulnerability to myself, and armoring up. I learned how to rationalize most situations, and how to tell people what this rationalization was.

At the same time, I learned that conflict was something to be navigated at my peril. My parents had an open marriage, which I thought was the way all marriages operated until, at the age of eight, I traveled for a month with my grandfather. One day, I offhandedly mentioned that my dad had a boyfriend, as did my mother, and that they regularly stayed the night. For the rest of the month, my grandfather casually asked me questions, trying to glean an understanding of this very foreign picture.

Upon our return, my grandfather confronted my parents and, once they confirmed it was true, stopped speaking to them entirely, refusing to enter our house or visit for any family occasion. For the next five years, the once inseparable relationship I had with my grandfather was conducted via parcels full of presents left on our doorknob and stealthy visits to my schoolyard. My sense of helplessness, anger, and bewilderment was further fueled by my mother's refusal to deal with the situation and my father's rage and blame.

Perceiving I couldn't express my feelings for fear of being made wrong in my vulnerability and only knowing how to deal with conflict by fighting, withdrawing, or making someone else wrong didn't help me build relationships. While people often confided in me, I always felt compelled to provide an answer to their problems, regardless of their perspectives or desires. Having equated knowing and telling as *the* way to show care and love, I couldn't understand why people I loved sometimes kept their distance from me.

By my mid-twenties, starved for true intimacy and connection, I knew there had to be a better way. But I didn't know what it was or where to find it. I felt like everyone else had been given an instructional manual or a roadmap for life that I wasn't privy to. And, I wanted in on it. This led me to complete Co-Active™ Coaching training, read hundreds of self-help and parenting books, complete emotional intelligence and leadership courses, and do a lot of self-reflection and hard self-work.

A marriage and a divorce later, I found myself in another relationship with a man who was also very good at telling me that whatever I felt was wrong. While this pattern was recognizable and felt like love as I had always known it, it no longer felt right or welcome. Breaking away from this intimately familiar and horribly constricting and destructive relationship was one of the hardest things I ever did. It also opened the gateway for me to meet my current husband, Olivier, with whom I could practice new ways of being and dealing with intimacy and conflict.

Our relationship isn't perfect. Like many couples, we fight about household chores, schedules, money, and whatever other petty things represent our deeper fears and tender spots. Our relationship is, however, heartfelt and supportive. Olivier's heart is huge. He wants connection and love more than he fears vulnerability, and he's committed to working to get it. Ultimately, he's a team player, and he's taught me the power of accepting someone unconditionally. It's taken us both a lot of vulnerability, exposure, and work to get to this place. And, we've both grown and continue to grow from it.

Matt grew up in an environment that adopted a completely different approach to relationships and conflict.

As the third and last child and the only boy, I was a golden child who could do no wrong. My environment was so pleasant and enjoyable, and I felt so accepted, that the only identity I developed for myself was that I was good, someone whom everyone liked and wanted to be around. This self-perception was constantly reinforced by people outside my family who would tell me how cute I was. By the time I was a teenager, I never rebelled because everything seemed pleasant and easy. Even though I hadn't done anything to deserve it, I had already started cruising through my life with an inflated ego and an attitude that I was a big deal.

Despite feeling accepted, judgment was ever-present in my household. As a result, I had also learned not to disagree with anyone, including my parents, and to avoid conflictual conversations. Disagreement meant getting into trouble, which I hated to do. I wanted to keep the peace with everyone so they would keep liking me.

Despite my skill in avoiding confrontation, even I couldn't avoid lying on occasion and getting called out for it. As a child, I loved to throw things, especially rocks, and could do it for hours on end. One day, my buddy and I were throwing rocks against a house in our neighborhood when we heard a loud bang and shattering glass. Naturally, we ran away. That evening, the phone rang during dinner. Once my mother got off the phone, she asked me, "Were you throwing rocks at the house across the street?" and I said, "No." This went on for several rounds after which my mother, knowing full well I was guilty, sent me to my room as punishment. Once there, I went to sleep, perceiving the storm would blow over by the time I woke up. Withdrawing by going to sleep was one of the first conflict avoidance techniques I knowingly developed, and it worked so well that I carried it over into adulthood.

By the time I was in my twenties, I'd developed severe social anxiety and my conflict avoidance strategies were well-honed. In my first fight with my wife, Susie, she eventually told me, "You need to go downstairs and sleep on the couch." As I slunk downstairs with my tail between my legs, I plopped myself on our couch, grateful that I'd at least get a good night's sleep. Susie woke me up five minutes later asking, "What are you doing?" When I told her I was sleeping, she stated, "We need to create a ground rule that we'll never go to bed angry and always work things out beforehand." We've managed to do this ever since.

Despite my attempt to start engaging with others when I had a different thought or perspective, because of my experience growing up of conflict as a win/lose proposition, I had a deeply engrained belief that the cost of losing a conflict (even one as simple as a difference of opinion) meant losing the relationship. As a result, I continued to avoid anything that might create friction. When my parents wanted something different from what Susie and I wanted, such as spending time together, I would agree to everything and everyone out of fear of disappointing someone, eventually disappointing them all anyway. My unwillingness to have clear conversations, sweeping many small and large conflicts under the rug, and my lying by omission had huge ramifications.

By the time I was in my mid-thirties, I realized I had some work to do and that if I didn't do it, I risked losing my wife, my three small children, and my family of origin. Working with Susie, my parents, and a family counselor, I realized how much of a role my lack of desire to engage in conflict had played in creating my family's dysfunction. I also realized how much I wanted to share my truth with my parents and that I had stopped myself from doing so out of fear that my parents only wanted to hear the truth as they saw it and receiving a different perspective would cause them to judge me. When it came down to it, I was fearful of disappointing them and of becoming the black sheep of the family, no longer the golden boy who could do no wrong.

As Susie and I continued to work together to address our issues honestly and head on, I began to realize how burying my own wants and needs had led me to become a people pleaser, and how my conflict avoidance patterns had led to thousands of missed conversations and opportunities over my lifetime. Determined to turn things around, I started taking more proactive steps towards embracing conflict and staying in it with my wife, my family, and my friends. Over time, I became more skilled at this and started creating small shifts in my relationships that had seismic impacts.

Although our upbringings were quite different, both Matt and I have been on long-time journeys to improve our relationships by upgrading our communication and conflict management skills. While we've both had some successes, until more recently, it was largely a random process of trial and error. This changed when we developed the HTI (Hearts Together Inspire) Relationship Map and started using it and its tools to understand our own and each other's preferences, values, and tendencies. This understanding helped us create alignment and work through conflict in a healthier, more productive, systematic manner. It brought us closer together as business partners and as friends.

As each of us became more familiar with the HTI Relationship Map and its tools, we started applying them to our other relationships. In all instances, this led to more intimacy, greater alignment, more streamlined and productive conflict, and better results. Ultimately, the HTI Relationship Map has helped us approach our relationships and conflict in a more empowered and systematic fashion and improved the likelihood of achieving our desired results as we and our partners emerge stronger together. When we started sharing these techniques with others (teams, families, small businesses, and large corporations), they began referencing the HTI Relationship Map, applying its tools, and experiencing significant shifts in their relationships and leadership. By using the HTI Relationship Map and applying its tools, you too will find your relationships and leadership transformed.

What is the HTI (Hearts Together Inspire) Relationship Map?

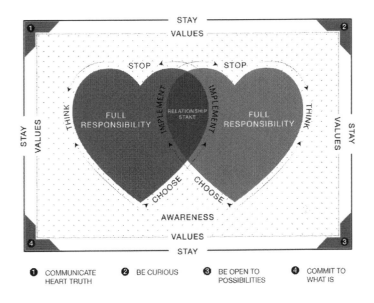

❶ COMMUNICATE HEART TRUTH   ❷ BE CURIOUS   ❸ BE OPEN TO POSSIBILITIES   ❹ COMMIT TO WHAT IS

The HTI Relationship Map[2] is like a geographical map in that it allows us to orient ourselves as to where we are. It also helps us see where we are in relation to ourself and others. The HTI Relationship Map helps us plot our relationships and use our pinpoint location as a base from which we can navigate and move forward together.

Without a map, without a shared stake and a commitment to stay in our relationship, and without expressed values to align to when things get difficult, it's often impossible to achieve efficient progress, meaningful purpose, and life-enriching movement. The HTI Relationship Map provides us with

---

2. You can download a free full color PDF of the HTI Relationship Map at www.htiinstitute.com/resources.

boundaries for the landscape we want to navigate, portrays the lay of our land, and provides us with navigational tools to get us to where we want to be, together.

Who Should Use the HTI Relationship Map?

Relationships are fluid; change is constantly happening within us, to us, and around us. We may find it easy to reach our goals and experience shared happiness and fulfillment in times of joy. Our relationships' dynamic natures, however, mean we may also find it easy to get lost, especially when conflict or confusion emerges. No matter our conditions, referencing the HTI Relationship Map to orient ourselves is advantageous since we journey through life in relationship with others. The Map helps us articulate where we are now and our desired destination and provides us with guidance and navigational choices to help us get there.

Easy to access and use, the HTI Relationship Map is designed for anyone who's in relationships, exposed to conflict, and has a vested interest in strengthening their relationships and increasing their ability to make an intentional impact. Essentially, it's for anyone who wants to get better at managing conflict, improve their relationships, achieve specific goals, and become an exceptional leader. This includes co-workers, teams, supervisors, managers, executives, parents, co-parents, couples, families, friends, lawyers, doctors, therapists, counselors, coaches, teachers, administrators, politicians, and organizations.

By navigating together towards an intentional destination, we enable and create a life-enriching experience of being in positive relationship. Through the ongoing process of navigating through conflict together, while staying in relationship with one another, we're able to come out on the other side with a relationship that's deeper and stronger than ever.

Key Points

- Relationships we have with ourself and others matter; they shape our experiences, provide us with meaning, and allow us to be impactful.
- Effective leadership requires positive relationships.
- Leadership isn't rank, title, or assignment. Leadership is an inside job and is about the thoughts, behaviors, and actions we choose.
- The HTI Relationship Map helps us pinpoint where we are in any given relationship at any point in time.
- When at a crossroads, in conflict, or at a place of choice, the HTI Relationship Map helps us identify our position, examine our options, and make a choice so we can create with intention and arrive at our desired destination, together.

Putting Concepts into Practice

Practice #1

Journal about yourself as a leader. You have many different roles and responsibilities in your life. Describe each role and how you show up as a leader in the role. How would you describe your leadership style? How would the people around you describe your leadership impact? For which roles in your life do you not show up as a leader and why?

Practice #2

Step 1: Draw an outline of the HTI Relationship Map without the two hearts. Think of a relationship that's important to you. Draw two hearts onto the map: the heart on the left represents you, and the heart on the right represents the other person.

Step 2: What do you notice? What size is each heart? If the hearts you drew connect and overlap, what does this mean to you? If the hearts are apart, disconnected and not touching, what does this represent? What are you becoming aware of based on your sketch?

Practice #3

Think about a challenging relationship that's important to you. Think about how you'd like it to look in the future. Think about what you're contributing to the current situation. What's preventing you from being in positive relationship with the other person and having the impact that you desire? List five thoughts, feelings, or actions you can shift to move your relationship to your ideal future state.

We always have a choice: how much choice we have in any situation is based on our perspectives and interpretations.

CHAPTER TWO

Full Responsibility

We aren't responsible for everything we're in relationship with. In fact, most of the time, what's happening outside ourselves is beyond our control. For example, the weather is ever-changing and we're always in relationship with it, regardless of whether we want to be or not. We are not, however, responsible for what it does, and we certainly cannot control it. What we can control and what we are responsible for is how we respond to it.

Similarly, in any relationship, we can't control the other person. Sometimes, we can't even choose the relationships we find ourselves in. For example, we can't choose our family of origin and, while many of us can choose our place of work, we can't always choose our co-workers. What we can do, however, is choose to take full responsibility in the following four distinct areas:

1. Ourself
2. Our impact on others
3. Our impact on our relationships
4. The impact our relationships have on our world

What Is Full Responsibility? Is It the Same as Fault?

Recently, Olivier and I went away to Vancouver Island for a romantic long weekend. The afternoon we were scheduled to leave, I was getting excited and wrapping up my work when he called to let me know an extreme windstorm was delaying sailings and we had a slim possibility of getting on the ferry that night. After discussing it, we decided to take our chances. I packed our car and we left for the ferry terminal as soon as he got home from work. An hour later, the gate flagger told us we had no hope of getting on that evening and we should turn around and try again in the morning. And so, we did a one-eighty, drove home for another hour and a half through Vancouver's gridlocked rush-hour traffic, and finally settled on an early bedtime to get up before dawn in hopes of making the 8:00 am ferry.

Olivier and I have fundamentally different approaches to waking up. I start moving as soon as my eyes open and my feet hit the ground, whereas Olivier moves slowly, needing time and coffee to get his motor running. When our alarm went off at 5:00 am, I rolled over, picked up my phone to check the ferry situation, and realized we needed to move quickly.

I nudged Olivier urgently, "Babe, we need to rock and roll. The 8:00 am is already full and we'll be lucky to make the ten o'clock – it's 65% full already."

"Ok. I'll go make my coffee and then we can go," he said sleepily.

"I think we should go now. We can get you a coffee at the ferry terminal."

"No way. It won't take me long. I'm not going without my coffee. Besides, it won't make any difference." And he shuffled off to the kitchen to make an espresso.

By the time we reached the ferry terminal forty minutes later, we were both cranky. I had a sneaking suspicion we weren't going to make the next ferry and had silently started blaming Olivier. As we stopped for the flagger, he told us we'd be lucky to make the 10:00 am ferry and were more likely to be boarding the 1:00 pm ship.

"Great, we're going to be spending the day in this parking lot," Olivier muttered grumpily as he drove down our assigned lane.

"Wait, I think you're in the wrong lane. The guy directed you to go into lane eight. No seriously, if we stay in lane nine, we won't have any chance at all. Can you move over?" I asked.

"It's too late. Anyway, it won't make any difference. There's no way we're going to make it onto this one." As Olivier looked at me, he added defensively, "I know you think it's my fault, but the five minutes it took me to make my coffee didn't make any difference. I drove really quickly, and we'd be even more behind if we'd taken your route."

As we sat in line, I was fuming. By the time the ten o'clock ferry began loading, I was steaming but holding onto hope that we'd make it onto the boat. As we inched forward, my heart lifted only to plummet down to earth as we approached the start line and the gate behind the last boarding vehicle came down in our faces. Lane eight was empty and we'd missed the sailing by one car. As I looked at Olivier with a scowl on my face, he uttered darkly, "It's not my fault."

Feeling like I was about to explode, I muttered, "I'm going to the washroom" and headed out for a walk, likely trailing clouds of irritated fumes in my wake. Once I'd circled the block a few times, I met up with Olivier along the ocean's bank and suggested we grab a bite to eat.

After sitting down, eating breakfast, and drinking a cup of coffee, our tempers settled, and we were able to think with clearer heads and hearts. Looking at each other sheepishly, we apologized for blaming each other for everything that had unfolded and started to ask ourselves what we could do differently to avoid going down a similar road in the future. Through the lens of identifying where we could each take ownership for what had occurred, we were able to unpack what had happened, where we'd gone wrong, where we'd failed to take responsibility, and find, together, more productive ways of moving forward that didn't include blame.

Although some people may think of fault when they think of responsibility, fault and responsibility aren't the same. Responsibility refers to owning our impact and the choices we make. Full responsibility is defined as owning the situation and/or relationship we find ourselves in, owning our part in contributing to it, owning our impact, and doing whatever we can, within our power, to address a problem or make an improvement. Full responsibility is based on the idea that we can control 100% of ourself, and 100% of our impact on any relationship we're in, regardless of whether or not we're in it by choice.

Taking full responsibility for a situation or relationship doesn't mean accepting we're to blame (i.e., "I caused it"). In fact, taking full responsibility never involves engaging in blame, fault finding, or using avoidance tactics. Because we're human, however, these responses are often part of our lives and relationships. We can and do make mistakes. Taking full responsibility involves recognizing when we're playing the blame game and recovering to a place where we can create what we desire.

Doing this often involves working with another person to look at ways we can solve the problem together. And, if that's not possible, looking for ways we can use our influence and resources to solve the problem. No matter what happens or how someone responds to us, we can always choose to find our heart, be in the present moment, reflect on past behaviors, thoughts, and actions, while keeping focused on our responsibility.

Full Responsibility for Self

The longest and most continuous relationship we'll ever have in our lifetime and the one that has the greatest impact on us is the one we have with ourself. It's ever-present and impacts how we feel about ourself, how we approach situations, the relationships we engage in, and the outcomes we create. It's also the relationship over which we have the most control. As Viktor Frankl, a noted Holocaust survivor, highlighted in his book *Man's Search for Meaning*, no matter what situation we find ourselves in or how little control we have over it, we can always access the power of choice to inform our reality and our relationship with ourself. Our perspective is a choice, and we can choose a different perspective at any time. As Dr. Wayne Dyer famously said, "When you change the way you look at things, the things you look at change." The oft-cited description of optimism versus pessimism as viewing the glass as half-full or half-empty illustrates this perfectly. While the glass always contains the same amount of liquid, changing our perspective immediately changes our experience of it and our experience in relation to it.

Similarly, we can change our perspective about our level of ownership of and responsibility for any given situation. The perspective we choose (full responsibility or less than full) has a significant impact. It impacts our feelings, energy, mindset, mood, behaviors, and our relationship with ourself. Once we've changed our perspective, the next step is to choose actions we'll take to impact our current situation so it falls more in line with the reality we want to create. This step is harder since it often requires us to surrender our ego, own our mistakes, and stay open and curious to someone else when we'd rather assign blame or find fault.

When I first moved from the East Coast to the West Coast, for example, I couldn't understand why everyone complained about the relentless months of gray and rain. From my perspective, rain was kind of cozy and way better than the mounds of snow and slush I was used to wading through daily. In fact, I used to quip about how I was now able to walk my dog without first having to put on a traveling sleeping bag and dig my car out of snow for half an hour only to find out it wasn't mine.

Fifteen years in as a West Coast resident, my attitude had changed somewhat. I was getting impatient with our gray skies and lack of sunshine and was constantly crabby. Going to hot yoga and lying on the floor with my eyes closed while imagining I was on a white sand beach wasn't cutting it. I was hating the West Coast, blaming it for all my misery as I dreamed of escaping to Mexico or the Caribbean for the winter months, if not forever. I wasn't liking myself or my attitude much in those days and neither was anyone else.

Finally, a friend told me they thought I had SAD (Seasonal Affective Disorder) and suggested I get a blue light to help treat it. Realizing I could take some steps to change my perspective and my relationship with myself, I started using one on a regular basis and noticed that not only did my attitude shift considerably but I started feeling better about myself and more empowered to create my reality. Eventually, I was once again able to appreciate the benefits of Vancouver's rain.

We can own and choose to be fully responsible for our history, our present, our future, our thoughts, our perspectives, our actions, our reactions, our beliefs, our desires, our aspirations, our feelings, our health (mental, physical, emotional, spiritual, financial), and our overall well-being. The starting point is identifying what's currently going on and making a choice to take full responsibility for it. No matter what. From this perspective, everything is possible, and we can create the world and relationships we want to experience, regardless of the situations or relationships we find ourselves in. While it takes work to master the skill of taking full responsibility for ourself and the circumstances we find ourselves in, doing so allows us to examine our options and make clear choices that are more in alignment with our values, vision, and desires. This is empowering.

Full Responsibility for Our Impact on Another Person

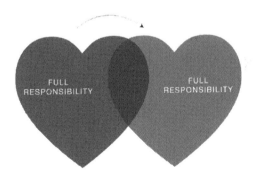

Each of us impacts the people and things around us. Sitting alone in a room, we impact the room's air, space, temperature, and energy. When someone else enters the room, they have an impact on the room and on us, as we do on them. No matter what we do, where we are, and who we're interacting with, we're always having an impact. Sometimes we can choose the impact we want to have, and sometimes we can't.

When we're in relationship with someone, no matter how fleeting the relationship, we're always impacting and influencing them. Regardless of whether our impact is by design or by accident, we always have the choice to take full (100%) responsibility for that impact. Doing so requires being aware of the emotions, thoughts, and behaviors that are influencing us and the impact we are having.

Taking full responsibility is an internal game. It's a choice we make independent of everything around us. It doesn't involve anyone else, nor does it involve taking responsibility for anyone's actions, thoughts, feelings, or behaviors. What another person chooses to do is out of our control, and how they respond to and feel about us is their responsibility. Their actions, reactions, and emotions can, however, provide us with some cues as to our impact.

If another person's reactions aren't what we're expecting or we interpret them as negative, instead of finding fault or making the person wrong, we can use this as an opportunity to get curious about our impact. Getting curious about the other person, including their thoughts and emotions, helps us better understand how we are or aren't serving them and how we might be out of alignment with our own or our relationship's values, purpose, desires, or goals. We can use this information to course correct our behavior and thoughts to achieve the impact we want to have on the people we're in relationship with.

Over the years, for example, I've learned that my directness can be perceived as aggressiveness. In fact, my ex-husband used to complain that I wasn't very "fluffy." I've since learned to tone my directness down a bit with people I'm less familiar with. I'm human, though, and sometimes forget to soften my approach and only realize it when I'm met with closed body language or sidestepped conversations. When this happens, I try to clean up my mistake by using a softer approach that's guided by my mental imagery of a bunny rabbit laying a path of cotton balls in its wake. Often, circling back to add the required padding allows for the original conversation and relationship to unfold without further missteps.

Full Responsibility for Our Impact on Our Relationship

Every relationship has, at a minimum, three entities: ourself, the other person, and our relationship. Just as each of us has unique values, goals, and aspirations for ourselves, as well as independent ways of operating in the world, we create values, goals, and aspirations for our relationship and develop unique ways of operating when together. This is true for all relationships, no matter how many people are involved. Because of this, while a specific behavior may not have a negative impact on the other person, it may have an immediate or long-term negative impact on our relationship. Each of us is 100% responsible for our impact on our relationship.

Olivier and I, for example, have completely different tastes in music. I love music from the 70s, and he loves what I, with the little musical knowledge I possess, call head-banging music. We both like to go to live concerts and both of us would be happy to go to them with people who enjoy our respective types of music. However, we both know that if we only ever went to concerts with other people, this would eliminate any possibility of us coming together around music and, over time, negatively impact our relationship. Consequently, despite teasing each other about our bad musical tastes, we try to find concerts we can enjoy together so we can expand each other's horizons and grow into one another, both of which are long-term goals for us and our relationship.

Being fully responsible for our relationships as their own entities is also key to taking full responsibility. Each of us is 100% responsible for our relationship's success and failure and for maintaining its ongoing health. Professional tango dancers who appear to move seamlessly together exemplify this. Each dancer needs to take full ownership and responsibility for themselves in terms of learning the steps and creating an act of beauty. Not knowing or being uncertain about what comes next would have a negative impact on their partner and on the dance. Both dancers also need to take full responsibility for the dance by being aware of how their movements, pacing, and timing are impacting one another and adjust accordingly to ensure synchronicity is maintained. One leads and then the other takes over. If one stumbles or missteps, the other compensates to ensure the partnership and the dance itself remain flowing and intact. Both are fully responsible for making it work.

Like tango dancers, when we each take full responsibility for our relationships, recovery from mistakes and recovery to each other is easier. Being responsible for our relationship as an independent entity allows us to sense missteps and take corrective actions, without wasting time on fault or blame. When we're clear on the impact we're having and the impact we want to have, when we're willing to make the adjustments required to be in alignment, and when we're fully responsible for our relationship, we're able to create the relationships we want to have.

Once Matt and I decided to work together as partners for the Co-Active™ Leadership project, we were required to climb thirty feet in the air and walk, in tandem, across a rope. We did this while teaching a course we were asked to design in less than five minutes to our audience on the ground who watched with necks craned. To do this, we both had to be fully responsible for our relationship: the minute one of us stepped out of taking 100% responsibility for our impact on each other or our impact on our relationship, we tended to lose our balance on the rope and risked falling to the ground. Only by having an awareness of what the other person needed and by providing it (flexibility or strength) were we able to right ourselves and, together, successfully walk the line.[3] While this experience provided us with direct and immediate feedback as to when we weren't taking full responsibility for our impact, less physical interactions provide us with this same type of feedback. When we attune to this input, we can use it to make new choices around how we interact with others and create our desired outcomes.

---

3. You can view a video of Tanya and Matt walking the line at www.htiinstitute.com/resources/.

Full Responsibility for Our Relationship's Impact on Our World

Just as no person is an island, no relationship exists in a vacuum. Work environments are filled with people operating as unique relational entities (teams, managers, departments, divisions, executives, and companies), as are families and communities (sports teams, volunteer groups, religious groups). Each of these relationships impacts the environment and systems in which it exists: our thoughts, feelings, behaviors, and actions are seen and felt, impacting the wider world we inhabit.

When Josh was younger, we'd frequently go to the playground. As he immersed himself into his environment, losing himself in the pleasure of climbing structures, he didn't always listen when asked not to jump from heights. Sometimes, worried he might fall and hurt himself, I'd get panicky and raise my voice, hoping he'd eventually listen as I repeated my requests.

Instead, as my voice carried fear through the air, he'd often climb higher to get away. At the same time, other parents would become alarmed and, as their children began to tune into their parents' changing mood, tension would rise throughout the playground. It took me a while to realize the negative spiral I was creating with Josh, and the negative impact our relationship was having on others in our environment. Once I realized the impact we were having, I was able to choose to take a different tack. By lowering my voice and going over to Josh when making my request, his response changed, tension evaporated, and the playground's dynamic changed completely.

A similar pattern often exists in workplaces. When a manager and employee or two co-workers don't get along, each contributes to the relationship's dysfunction and both are impacted. The dysfunctional relationship also negatively impacts the office environment and people they interact with, often contributing to ill-health, more conflict, reduced productivity, and employee turnover. Taking full responsibility for our relationships' impacts requires having an awareness of how we and our partners move together and impact our environment, other people, other relationships, and the systems around us.

We can see how taking full responsibility impacts an organization's success in creating the relationships they want with their customers. When people see organizations and groups acting out of integrity with their values, their reputations eventually suffer. The inverse is also true.

As an organization, Patagonia, the outdoor garment company, made a commitment to keep clothing out of landfills. It promises to repair, reuse, and recycle garments that are beyond use. A while ago, my cousin in Seattle enthusiastically received me at the door when I arrived at her home. After asking how her day had gone, she told me, "It was amazing! You need to come and see what I got in the mail today."

She brought me to her dining room table, saying, "I bought a sweater from Patagonia twenty-five years ago and it's one of my favorites. I wear it every year. A couple of weeks ago, I pulled it out of my closet to pack it for our upcoming trip to the Norwegian fjords when I noticed some holes in it. So, I called Patagonia to find out what I could do, and they told me to send it to them." She pulled her sweater out of an envelope and showed me how Patagonia had not only repaired the holes but added two new matching patches, one on each arm, along with matching overlay stitching, giving it an updated and stylish look. Both she and I were incredibly impressed by how far above and beyond Patagonia had gone in terms of meeting its lifetime guarantee, environmental commitments, and customer service promises. Since then, I've become a convert to the idea of paying more for Patagonia's products, feeling like I'm buying into more than just a garment.

Taking full responsibility for our relationships' impact on the wider world is both a responsibility and an opportunity. Knowing where we have control and influence in and for our relationships and knowing where we can take responsibility and ownership is essential. Acting on this knowledge empowers us to make decisions that influence our relationship's trajectory (for example, adjusting our approach or staying the course regardless of obstacles encountered) and its impact on the wider world. It allows us to design and create the reality we operate in. It also ensures our relationships live and thrive in alignment with their values and purpose. Opportunities for us to engage in this process are endless.

Why Is Taking Full Responsibility Important?

Since change is constant, inevitable, and relentlessly in motion, conditions around and within our relationships are constantly in flux. Accepting this while taking responsibility for becoming skilled at navigating and adjusting to changes, both individually and as a partnership, allows us to serve everyone involved. Although we can take full responsibility in four distinct areas (self, others, our relationship, and our relationship in the world), rarely are they separate in real life. Taking responsibility in one area often means taking responsibility in another, even if unintentionally.

By 2007, Starbucks was in trouble. Its stock had fallen by 42%, its coffee had declined in quality, workers were disengaged, customers' orders were largely incorrectly filled, and many stores had lost their appeal as a third place (outside of home or work) where people could meet, socialize, and create community. In January 2008, Howard Schultz confronted this situation when he was brought back in as CEO.

After identifying Starbucks' negative impacts on its wider environment (communities, clients, investors, workers, and their families), Schultz set about to fix the problems. In February 2008, he closed all Starbucks stores for three and a half hours to retrain baristas on how to make the perfect espresso. Despite lost revenue, Schultz made these decisions knowing that if he didn't invest in his people, they couldn't invest in Starbucks' customers and deliver what was expected of them. He then made a commitment that all stores would grind their own beans and throw away any coffee sitting for longer than thirty minutes and doubled the amount of fair-trade coffee Starbucks purchased. These commitments were in line with Starbucks' value of being performance-driven, through the lens of humanity.

Schultz also hired outside consultants to help him figure out how to save the company money. Their first solution, the obvious and logical choice, was to get rid of Starbucks employees' full health benefits. This solution was out of alignment with his own and Starbucks' corporate values. Not only did Schultz refuse to entertain the idea, but he ensured that Starbucks provided all full- and part-time workers and their live-in partners with full medical benefits and granted all workers stock options. This was no small commitment given the high unemployment rate and global recession in effect at the time.

The impact of Schultz taking full responsibility for himself, his impact on his employees, and Starbucks' relationship with them was entire families felt that Starbucks cared for them as people. They also received a large measure of security in a time of great insecurity, when lack of access to healthcare benefits could spell personal financial disaster and ruin. Taking full responsibility and implementing these measures took courage and resulted in solidified and strengthened relationships.

As a final step, Schultz commissioned a design firm to redesign all of Starbucks' stores. He wanted them to be highly personalized and reflect the coffeehouse feel originally intended to attract people and create community. By taking these measures, Schultz took responsibility for the impact Starbucks as an entity was having on the wider community. Baristas were committed to providing top quality drinks to Starbucks' customers and to Starbucks fulfilling its vision and purpose. The stores became more inviting as a third space between work and home, thereby serving community needs. Extended health care and education opportunities benefitted workers' families. Starbucks also became very profitable, rewarding shareholders who had stuck with the company throughout the turmoil.

What's the Cost of Not Taking Full Responsibility?

Failing to take full responsibility for ourself and our relationships, their health, harmony, and disharmony, and own our impact comes with a very real cost. Opting to take less than 100% responsibility is a choice that involves giving away partial or full responsibility for who we are, the life we're living, and the future we're creating. This diminishes our own power and opens the door for blame, victimhood, and irresponsibility.

It also increases the probability that we'll disconnect from ourself and others, and that our relationships will fall apart. Disconnection can happen quickly, or slowly and subtly, as power struggles shift our relationship's focus from "we and us" to "you vs. me / me vs. you." This often shows up as one individual blaming the other. Focusing on who's at fault can weaken and polarize our relationships if resentment, feelings of being better than or less than, and other judgments fill our space and ego-fueled attention becomes our focus. Ultimately, any movement we make away from taking full responsibility for ourselves, our impact, and our relationships taints our relationships and limits our growth. It's also an inefficient use of energy, restricting what we can create, both individually and together.

Navigating our changing landscapes and conditions (changes in our environment, changes in our partners, changes in ourself) is sometimes simple and often complex. Being aware of how we can take full responsibility provides us with opportunities to impact our relationships' quality and experience. While mastering this takes work, not taking responsibility also takes work and is potentially more costly in terms of our energy expenditure, inability to adapt to change, and failed relationships.

What's the Benefit of Taking Full Responsibility?

Taking full responsibility allows us to act with intent and have a positive impact. Essentially, it provides us with a measure of control over ourself and our experience, helps us achieve or create our desired outcomes, and allows us to be the best possible version of ourself.

Claiming full responsibility for ourselves, our impacts, and our relationships also creates space and opportunities for us to willingly engage and live in a reality that results from making conscious choices. We can choose the degree of transparency, authenticity, commitment, and integrity we employ in our relationships. By making choices and taking responsibility for them, we place ourselves firmly in the driver's seat of our life: we are in control and always have the power to make new decisions.

Ultimately, choosing to take full responsibility in all four areas is a powerful combination that allows us to create hope, choice, and success. It unlocks potential, creates freedom, and empowers us in all our relationships. Our current reality is always the result of the sum of a multitude of decisions we've made in the past. Empowering ourselves to choose full responsibility allows us to exert influence and have an intentional impact on our relationships. Relationships that operate with intention are powerful.

Key Points

- Full responsibility means taking 100% ownership of what is within our control.

- We always have a choice. Choosing to take full responsibility is choosing to be empowered.

- We can take full responsibility for: 1) ourself, 2) our impact on others, 3) our impact on our relationships, and 4) the impact our relationships have on our world.

- Full responsibility can only be present when there is a complete absence of blame.

- Opting to take less than full responsibility (<100%) diminishes our power and negatively impacts our relationships.

- Claiming full responsibility empowers us to make conscious choices, be responsible for our impact, and intentionally create the world and relationships we want to be in.

Putting Concepts into Practice

Practice #1

Journal about your level of responsibility in your life. Think about a key relationship and describe its quality. Rate this quality on a scale of one to ten; one being awful – it's barely hanging on by a thread – and ten being amazing – exhilarating and on cloud nine. With your rating in mind, reflect on how you're contributing to this number. What are you responsible for and what are you not responsible for? Where and how can you take more responsibility for your impact and your relationship?

Practice #2

Sketch a cylinder and label it 0% (bottom) to 100% (top). Think of a relationship you're in that is operating at a level that's less than your ideal state. Draw a line to reflect the level of responsibility you feel you take in this relationship. For example, if you hold other people (for example, parents) or other factors (for example, country of origin, family history, etc.) as 50% of the reason for your circumstances, you'd draw a horizontal line at 50%. Reflect on what you can choose to take responsibility for and what you can change to move the line towards 100%.

Values provide us with guideposts for how to behave as we pursue our goals and help us create boundaries within which we want to operate.

CHAPTER THREE

Values

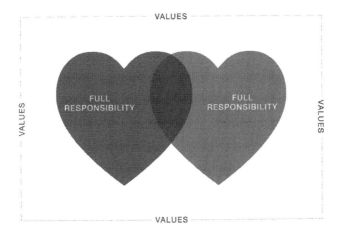

The HTI Relationship Map places a boundary around each relationship. This allows us to identify which relationship we're navigating, while clearly distinguishing it from all others. Having a distinct boundary allows our partnership to expand on purpose, with meaning, and with intent.

Values form our relationship boundary's inner core. Each person, as well as our relationship, has a unique set of values. From time to time, we may trample on individual or relationship values. And, it's possible for us and our relationship to recover. In fact, our connection is sometimes fostered and deepened through effectively resolving values conflicts. Ultimately, knowledge about and respect for our and our partner's values helps our hearts stay open to and in relation with one another. Because our and our relationship's values may change over time and are somewhat permeable, values are indicated on the HTI Relationship Map by a dotted line.

What Are Values?

Values are the elements we think are worthwhile and important in life – the things we value. They guide who we are and how we show up. Values are wide-ranging and can encompass a variety of characteristics. We can objectively measure some of them whereas others are entirely subjective. And, unlike moral imperatives (for example, don't lie or cheat), we don't apply them universally.

The following are a few examples of values:

Abundance	Integrity
Accomplishment	Logic
Achievement	Love
Adventure	Loyalty
Bravery	Minimalism
Comfort	Obedience
Consistency	Open-mindedness
Cooperation or collaboration	Patience
Creativity	Power

Education
Elegance
Empathy
Family
Fitness
Fluidity
Freedom
Frugality
Generosity
Health
Humility
Individualism

Privacy
Punctuality
Reason
Reliability
Responsibility
Safety
Self-actualization
Service
Tact
Truth
Wealth, etc.

Personal Values

Values are intensely personal. Each of us has a unique set of values reflecting our distinctive personalities and the belief systems we use to interpret our world. Some of us have given much thought to our values, can clearly articulate them, and intentionally model them through our behavior. Matt's values, for example, are "freedom, love, service, and inspiration." Mine are slightly different, expressed as "growth, integrity, love, and creativity." Others of us have personal values not yet articulated or expressed, even to ourselves. We may, for example, be drawn to certain experiences (for example, art openings), or environments (for example, natural settings untamed by humankind), and not know why, unaware we have strong values of beauty, creativity, and nature. Most of us have a mixture of clearly defined and assumed values. All of these inform who we are, how we behave, and what matters to us. They also influence how we feel in any given situation.

How we express our values is extremely personal and values underlying the same action may vary from person to person. For example, I make all our family's food from scratch and, for most of Josh's life, made sure we ate dinner together as a family. It's also important to me that I feed people visiting us with something I've made. One day, when Matt and I were talking about this, he asked me what was behind these desires. After thinking about it for a bit, I told him, a bit tongue in cheek, "I'm Jewish. Food is love and when you eat together, your relationship tends to grow. That's usually why, when Jews and families get together to celebrate, a chicken must die." When I thought about it some more, though, I realized that making food from scratch, often inventions of my imagination, honors my values of love and growth and is a way for me to express creativity. For Matt, providing dinner, whether he's cooking it himself or ordering in, honors his values of service and love. By doing so, he's also honoring his value of freedom since he's still free to contribute to his family at the end of his workday in one way or another.

Why Are Values Important?

Values typically inform where we want to focus our attention and energy, what our priorities are, and how we choose to behave. They often reflect how we aspire to be. This is as true for people as it is for organizations. Patagonia and Starbucks, for example, have strong value sets that guide their decision-making and inform our experience of them.

Whether stated or unstated, our values act as our compass, moving us towards some experiences and away from others. My value of growth, for example, often prompts me to geek out and learn, resulting in an accumulation of several degrees and numerous certifications in areas that grab my interest, even if no obvious applicability or financial reward is attached. My value of creativity, on the other hand, inspires me to attend art and theater events, try my hand at painting pictures, and put myself out there in improv classes.

Values also help us establish our goals and make decisions. They can influence our choices by acting as a guiding principle or decision-making point when we're at a crossroad. When Matt first started looking at taking the Co-Active™ Leadership course, for example, he initially put it off, feeling the cost and time investment would take away from his ability to serve his family. Over time, however, his perception changed. As he leaned into his values of freedom and inspiration, he realized he could offer his family and others more of himself and be more inspiring if he gave himself the freedom to complete it. Leaning into these values eventually allowed him to make a new decision.

Our values inform us as to whether we're moving closer to or farther away from what's important to us and how well we're in alignment with them. Feelings of uneasiness or extreme discomfort, for example, often let us know one of our core values is being violated or that we're currently out of alignment with our values. We can be susceptible to these feelings in an instant or, gradually, over time.

Heeding these feelings of discomfort lets us know something in our current situation is less than optimal or that we're out of alignment and need to course correct. Ultimately, we can use these feelings as a reminder to:

- Slow down;
- Take inventory of what's going on;
- Investigate which of our values are being stepped on (by ourself or by others);
- Explore options for bringing ourself back into alignment.

This is an important process since we're often the best version of ourself when we're operating in alignment with our values.

Matt's story illustrates this well. *This morning I went into my kitchen to make myself something to eat. I walked towards the counter and noticed the floor was greasy and some bits of foil were lying around. As I was trying to figure out what was going on, I also noticed my dog had bits of foil stuck to him and his fur was matted. When I couldn't find the butter that should've been on the counter, I put two and two together and realized our dog had eaten the seven-dollar brick of organic butter Susie had just bought. By then, I was mad at the dog I had never wanted and I was frustrated with Susie, who probably left the butter close to the counter's edge where our dog could reach up and get it, even though she knows he doesn't listen very well and can't be trusted. As my frustration and irritation mounted, I started banging out a text message about it to her which, as you can imagine, wasn't particularly gentle or subtle.*

Part way through typing my message, I realized I was feeling uncomfortable, emotionally charged, and ill at ease, so I paused to breathe. Looking down at what I had written, I recognized my message in no way served anyone, wasn't likely to inspire change, and wasn't particularly loving. I was about to violate three of my core values. I deleted my message and decided to handle it another way. When Susie came home that night, I mentioned to her in passing what had happened. I also suggested she might want to be careful about pushing food left on the counter back towards the wall and she seemed to receive this well. Whether or not it happens again, at least I know I was leaning into my values and resolving the situation in a way I felt good about.

Ultimately, values provide us with guideposts for how to behave as we pursue our goals and help us create the boundaries we want to operate in. They also allow us to express our highest selves when we're living and acting in alignment with them.

Relationship Values

Since each of us is unique, our individual values are unique. This means for every relationship we're in, some or all of our values may overlap with our partner's. And, we may have one or more values that are at odds (for example, frugality vs. generosity). When in relationship, we may also share broader values and goals (for example, organizational, familial, religious) while differing on our personal ones.

Just as our relationships take on unique identities, patterns, movements, and goals, they also typically have their own values. Our relationship values exist side by side with our personal values and may align, partially overlap, or be entirely unique. For example, if you remember, Matt's personal values are "freedom, love, service, and inspiration" and mine are "growth, integrity, love, and creativity." Our business relationship's core values are "collaboration, possibilities, love, and integrity." We defined these together and, while they're slightly different from each of our personal value sets, they're in alignment with them.

The clearer we are on our individual and our relationship's values, the more likely we are to work in true partnership with one another. Knowing them also allows us to encourage each other to live into our values and support each other as we do so. One day, for example, when Matt was going off about something and well into a rant, I gently asked him, "How are you leaning into your value of love right now?" With this question, he was able to examine his words and thoughts, and choose different ones based on a new perspective that's more in line with his values.

How Can We Identify Our Values?

Identifying our values can be a simple exercise or a more complex one, depending on which values we're trying to pinpoint. Identifying our core values may initially seem easy. Once we dig a bit deeper, however, we sometimes discover our core values are different from ones we originally identified.

A great way to go about identifying our core values is to come up with a comprehensive list of what's important to us. Thinking about the following can help us complete this process:

- A peak experience you had, one where everything was flowing perfectly and you lost sense of time and space, melding perfectly into the moment. What was happening? Which values were you honoring?

- A time when you became extremely angry or agitated. What was happening? What rubbed you the wrong way? Which of your values were violated?

- What do you admire in yourself or others in terms of ways of being in the world? What values does this conduct represent or reflect?

Reflecting on our answers to these questions allows us to mine our memories for our values and create a laundry list of everything that shows up. After we've come up with a complete list of values that are important to us, the next step involves bucketing them into related groupings. Once groupings emerge, we can select our top value, the one most accurately reflecting our truth or standing above the rest. This value becomes our core value and represents all others in the group. My value of integrity, for example, includes values of transparency, truth, acting for the highest good, serving, acting in alignment with my words, modeling integrity to inspire others, and doing my best in all situations. Integrity is the catch-all word, reminding me of everything I value and driving my decision-making when I'm operating at my best.

Repeat this process until three or four core values are identified. It's important to keep this list short since a longer core values list tends to become diluted and is less effective in terms of providing guidelines for our behavior and decision-making.

Conflict

No matter what type of relationship we're in, respecting the values of those with whom we're in relationship, even if we don't hold them ourself, is important. While we don't have to like someone else's values or even agree with them, we do have to respect that they're important to them and that they reflect a fundamental truth about them. Accepting someone's values is part of accepting who they are. Doing so helps us build connection and trust. On the flip side, failing to honor or respect someone's values often leads to conflict, disagreements, and misalignment.

In a team that I worked with, for example, meetings consistently went over their scheduled time, and this created conflict. Sue, one of the team members, always left at the meeting's scheduled end time whereas the rest of the team would stay until the meeting had completed, regardless of how much extra time was expended. Jess, the team leader in charge of overseeing the meetings, became increasingly frustrated with Sue, perceiving her as lacking commitment. Tension between the two increased over time, eventually spilling over and creating a divisive team atmosphere. Once the two of them talked, Sue explained that respect for time was one of her core values. Consequently, it was important to her to honor her commitments to the team and to other people she'd scheduled meetings with. Leaving on time allowed her to do this. Jess, on the other hand, had a value of giving 100%. For her, giving 100% translated into staying in the meeting until everything was resolved, regardless of scheduled time limits. Once Sue and Jess realized they were having a values conflict, they were able to approach the issue from a different angle and resolve it in a way that honored both their values. This resolved the conflict, improved team morale, and allowed for greater productivity.

If one person in our relationship relinquishes any of their values to be present, participate, or make the other person happy, our relationship is likely to operate on a superficial level. Because it's hard to find alignment and shared collaboration in an "either/or" or "win/lose" situation, our relationship's strength and integrity are compromised if we don't address the imbalance. For our relationships to thrive, each person's values need to be acknowledged and respected.

Our values also inform our decision-making and how we respond to conflict. Stepping back and looking at our values, our partner's values, and our relationship's values before responding to a conflict increases the likelihood that we'll act in alignment with our values while respecting our partner's. It also helps us avoid making assumptions about the motivations behind someone's behavior or assigning meaning to specific actions. Getting curious about our partner's and our relationship's values helps us avoid making up a meaning for something based on our own knowledge and biases, something that often results in negative storytelling and even more conflict.

Matt's and my differing approaches to our work commitments, for example, were almost a deal breaker. When we first started working together, we set up a regular working schedule. Sometimes, Matt would send me a text at the last minute abruptly telling me plans had changed and announce a new start time. I began to find this grating since my value of integrity means that when Matt and I book time to work together, I'll often say no to anything interfering with this commitment and schedule anything new around it. For Matt, leaning into his value of freedom or service sometimes means if something comes up that he believes will add more to our business or something else that's important to him, or if he needs to fulfill an obligation for his family, he'll try to reschedule our time.

If I consistently accommodated Matt's value of freedom at the expense of my value of integrity or vice-versa, our relationship might appear to be working. Over time, however, whoever was continually sacrificing their value for the sake of harmony would likely feel resentful about being unimportant and disrespected. Our relationship would probably become rife with dissention and strife. And so, even though I found it uncomfortable, I broached the subject with Matt. We overcame the issue by having an open conversation that allowed us to come to a better understanding of each other and our personal values and develop our relationship in a positive direction. By taking time to find out what was motivating each of our behaviors and the values that underlie them, and by regularly talking about this issue as it arises instead of reacting to it, Matt and I are able to circumvent a lot of conflict that would otherwise ensue, even though these direct conversations can feel uncomfortable.

At every point in our relationships, we have a choice as to how to respond when conflict arises. Noticing when we or someone else is having a strong reaction to something often tells us there's a values conflict or that one or more value is being trampled on. We can try to untangle our and our partner's motivations from our behaviors and act in a way that's in alignment with our values or we can react to the conflict's content and risk acting outside of our values.

Remaining connected to our values and in a heart-centered relationship is important, regardless of a conflict's content. It requires us to be conscious of our actions relative to our relationship and be aware of our actions' impact on the other person as well as on our relationship. Trust in the other person and in our relationship is established and eroded based on how much we behave and respond in a way that's in alignment with our own values, our partner's values, and our relationship's values.

Integrity

Acting in alignment with our values is a way we exhibit integrity. On occasion, however, we may have an internal conflict between two of our values. Over the past years, for example, I've frequently experienced a conflict between my values of love and growth. As a single mom for over a decade, I was solely responsible for taking care of Josh. Although I wouldn't have had it any other way, there were many times when I was confronted with growth opportunities I wanted to engage in that would also have required that I take large chunks of time away from Josh and sacrifice my value of love. As a result of having to pick honoring one value over another, I often experienced tension during this period of my life.

We may also experience conflict between two competing expressions of the same value. My value of love, for example, means spending time with my family, especially with Olivier and Josh, is important to me. My value of love also means I feel the need to protect my own boundaries as a form of self-love when I feel overloaded. This can create tension in my relationships with my family. If I sacrifice my own boundaries out of feelings of obligation or guilt, I can begin to feel resentful and powerless.

Sacrificing one or more of our values out of guilt or obligation, even if the purpose is to honor another value, often makes us feel like we're out of alignment with our values, powerless, and a victim. This is especially true if we're doing this unconsciously or to meet someone else's expectations. It's the opposite of taking full responsibility. Making a conscious choice as to the value we're choosing to honor and owning our choice, including what we're saying yes and no to, allows us to feel powerful, stay in integrity, and take full responsibility for ourself and our relationships. It also creates space for a conversation in which we and our partners can gain clarity and a deeper understanding of what's important to us and why we're making our choices. These openings are relationship gold and allow our relationships, with ourself and with others, to remain in integrity.

Recovery

Just as values are sometimes a source of conflict, they're also a place we can recover to, individually and together.

Since our life is experienced as a series of relationships with people, places, and things, and because the quality of our life is measured by the quality of our relationships, establishing a boundary around how we choose to experience our life and relationships is extremely valuable. Having clearly defined values allows us to create a distinct boundary around each of our relationships, helping us keep them intact as they grow. Values also serve as our personal and relationship guides by providing fodder from which we can envision, design, build, and renovate our life and relationship experiences while informing the quality and quantity of decisions we make to bring our vision to life.

While we can't control everything around us, at any given moment we can choose to be intentional and proactive with our thoughts, actions, and behaviors. We can set out to create our life and step intentionally into and in alignment with our values. When life happens to us, seemingly without rhyme or reason, we always have the power to choose how we'll react and respond and move forward in alignment with our values. Choosing to do so is a powerful way to intentionally navigate and thrive. It's exponentially more powerful when we choose to do it together.

Key Points

- Values are an expression of what we prioritize as worthwhile and important in life.
- Explicitly defined or not, everyone has a personal set of core values.

- Every relationship has a set of unique values in addition to each person's individual values.

- Values guide where we place our focus, attention, and energy and help guide our thoughts, behaviors, feelings, decisions, and actions.

- Knowing, understanding, and respecting our own values and our partner's helps our hearts stay open to and in relation with one another.

- We can use values as a compass to navigate our lives and relationships with integrity.

- Our values inform our decision-making and how we respond to and create from conflict.

Putting Concepts into Practice

Practice #1

Step 1: Write down twenty-five values that are important to you. Don't overthink it, simply write twenty-five key words that represent what you value.

Step 2: You may notice some similar words. For example, you may have written down trust and then written down safety. Begin to group similar words/values or ones you feel belong together.

Step 3: For each grouping, select the word/value that you feel best represents the rest of the ones in the group.

Step 4: Select your top four values/groupings.

Step 5: Write a paragraph about what these four values mean to you. Why are they important and how do you model them?

Practice #2

Think of a role model or a mentor whom you admire and respect.

Step 1: Describe their actions and behaviors you admire and write down ten words that describe them (for example, confident, trustworthy, energetic, creative, faithful, dynamic, hard working, competitive, resilient, brave, etc.).

Step 2: Which four core values do you believe shape their decision-making, choices, actions, and behaviors?

Practice #3

Step 1: Look up your company's core values and write them down exactly as your company displays them.

Step 2: In your words, write down what they mean to you.

Step 3: Describe a time when one of your co-workers modeled these values. Describe a situation when you know these values were not being honored.

Step 4: How do you model these values? What are three examples from last week?

By staying in our relationship, keeping our hearts open, and displaying vulnerability without armoring up, we can navigate our conflict, better understand one another, and find a third way of moving forward, together.

CHAPTER FOUR

Stay

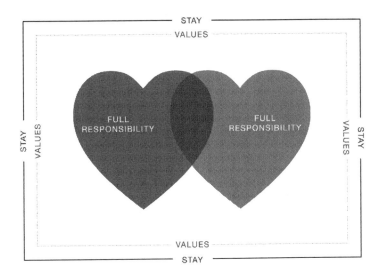

Humans are dynamic and relationships are fluid. Stay refers to the necessity of remaining in relationship with ourself and another, regardless of changes, obstacles, and conflict encountered if we want our relationship to grow and thrive. Staying or leaving, however, is always a choice.

In the HTI Relationship Map, stay creates the periphery of our relationship's boundary, formalizing and containing it as a unique entity. Stay is drawn as a solid outer line because, while respecting each other's values is important for our relationships to thrive, it's not enough. Having a solid container protects our relationship, reducing the likelihood that its original partnership will be impacted by outside forces while preventing it from becoming unbounded or slipping away.

Choosing to stay in our emotions, in our current situation, and in our relationship, even when we're uncomfortable, gives us the greatest chance of yielding the best outcome for ourselves and those around us. Staying in alignment with who we are and what matters to us, while respecting the person we're in relationship with, allows our authentic self to emerge. Staying connected to and centered in ourself is the best stepping-stone to being in positive and healthy relationship with others. This is all the more true when conflict is present.

Natural Responses to Conflict

I was working as a consultant in a large utilities company to institute non-negotiable safety practices. This was a huge culture change. The room was packed with trades instructors who would be required to deliver safety training and then assess their peers. Failure to pass an assessment meant a temporary suspension from work and a loss of wages until the person could be retrained, be reassessed, and pass. Not only were we asking instructors to deliver training in a more consistent and prescribed manner than they were used to, but we were asking them to go back and work side by side with the people they were assessing, regardless of pass or failure.

As we reviewed the requirements with them, instructors and union representatives were twitchy and on edge. Some of them could barely look me in the eye. Although they were turning pages and appeared to be following our explanations of what was required, it was clear we were approaching something that resembled a mutiny. As tension reached a breaking point, I asked, "What's going on? It's clear no one's happy. What's the elephant in the room?"

As I looked around the room, almost no one would meet my gaze. The silence began taking on a deafening resonance of its own. Finally, one instructor, with shoulders so tense his ears almost disappeared inside them, looked up, found my eyes, and bravely said, "I think this project is important – it's going to save lives. And, I don't like that we need to teach from this guide. It feels like I need to memorize lines and I'll be judged and penalized if I forget some. I also feel really uncomfortable about assessing and potentially failing guys I know can do the work and whom I need to work with in the future. In fact, I hate it."

By staying in the situation and in his emotions, and sharing them with the group, he allowed everyone in the room to do the same and opened the door for discussion to take place. As fears, concerns, and hopes were aired and addressed, the group decided to make a commitment to stay with the project and, although uncomfortable, try this new way of doing their job. In the end, the project was a huge success – lives were and continue to be saved, instructors grew their skill sets, and new conversations and ways of doing business were set as a precedent. By committing to stay the course, regardless of what showed up, instructors created the conditions in which growth, connection, trust, and greater results occurred. All of these allowed them to be better leaders in the classroom and in the field and produced more effective results.

As humans, our natural inclination is to see conflict, or its source, as a threat. This is our survival instinct and it's hardwired in us. Historically, as a species, when encountering a threat, we've used one of two default responses: fight or flight. And, both worked impressively well when we encountered an obvious threat, such as a saber-toothed tiger or a lion roaming the savanna.

In more modern times, however, threats we encounter or perceive aren't always so evident. They're often more subtle and caused by change and interpersonal differences. Consequently, the lizard part of our brain responsible for our fight or flight response has become more sophisticated and we've evolved to react to threatening stimuli with one of the following response patterns:

1. *Fight* – a classic win/lose situation where the person with the most power usually wins the conflict at everyone else's expense.

2. *Flight* – a lose/lose situation in which the conflict has no hope of resolving itself and the relationship is negatively impacted, suspended, or terminated.

3. *Freeze, deny or ignore* – freezing, ignoring the conflict or denying there is one is a process in which conflict is rarely resolved, and often repeats or escalates quietly.

4. *Accommodate* – smoothing over the problem without addressing any underlying issues is a process that makes the current problem superficially disappear as it continues to live underground, often surfacing more frequently and with increasing intensity.

5. *Negotiate or compromise* – a process in which each person gives something up to come to a mid-point solution that may address the problem, but to which no

one is truly committed and relationship potential is impeded.

6. *Collaborate* – a process in which everyone stays standing in the stillness caused by the tension between chaos and silence to look for a third way (different from my or your way) that solves the problem and is agreeable to and beneficial for all, including the relationship itself.

As a process, change often involves disagreement, tension, and escalated conflict. The first five approaches may resolve an immediate problem. When faced with ongoing friction, however, working collaboratively through the discomfort associated with our shifting relational atmosphere is the only way to create positive and lasting change. Doing this requires that we stay.

What Is "Stay" and What Does It Look Like?

Unlike Pavlovian stimulus-responses observed in dogs and other animals, we, as humans, are gifted with the ability to pause between stimulus and response and consciously decide how we want to respond. We can also choose to elongate the pause for as long as we need.

The pause provides us with an opportunity to stop and think so we can respond with intention, not merely react to our current situation or our conflict's content. It allows us to respond in a way that's more in keeping with who we are, what we believe in, our values, and what we desire. Because we often want to run away from conflict, staying is frequently the make-or-break-it factor, allowing us to respond with intentionality and create a firm relational foundation built on trust.

Staying requires we mentally and physically remain in the pause between stimulus and response while attempting to elongate the space between the two. Staying in the pause allows us to take a moment to pinpoint where we and our partner are in relation to each other (for example, Are we at an impasse? Are we near each other but not yet in sync?) and provides us with the possibility of developing an awareness of our environment, our values, the relationship we're in, and the outcomes we most long for. It also provides us with the space needed to distinguish between what our head and our heart are telling us is true and become curious about the person and situation in front of us. We can then use this new knowledge to choose to respond in line with our values and our hearts' innermost longings. In doing this, we often become closer to the person we want to be, the best version of ourself, and more authentic with the people we're in relationship with.

Staying also involves staying in our current situation and/or relationship, even when it's uncomfortable for us. This may involve staying physically and emotionally present in a conflict until we're able to recover. It requires maintaining a commitment to our relationship and to resolving our current situation, even if we need to take a breather in between. In this case, staying involves letting our partner know we're stepping away from our relationship and our current conflict for a period of time with the *aim* of returning to work through our conflict in a more productive and collaborative manner.

Olivier, for example, tends to get overwhelmed and flooded when there's conflict. His instinct is to leave, think about what's going on, assess his emotions and thoughts, and then come back to work things out. In our relationship's early days, though, I didn't know he was coming back and so, when things got hot and he clammed up or walked away, I would become increasingly frustrated and pursue him to engage. This caused him to shut down even more and, sometimes, physically leave our environment. Even though Olivier eventually came back to re-engage and work through whatever issue we were dealing with, this cycle added to our overall conflict.

As I observed this pattern over time, I brought it up with Olivier at which point he told me, "You know that when I get like that, I need time to think things through. You should know me well enough by now to know I'm always going to come back." As I reflected on his answer, I realized I didn't always know this was his intention or that he'd come back. As a result, I not only felt angst about our existing conflict but insecure about the direction our relationship was headed in. It was as if I was left with 200% responsibility for holding onto our relationship while he went rogue. I realized that if he had told me he just needed a breather to figure things out before moving forward and that he fully intended on coming back to work things out, my perspective and feelings would have shifted one hundred and eighty degrees. When I first explained this to him, he didn't understand why communicating this would make such a difference but agreed to try to do so moving forward and has kept to this.

Since then, the process we use and our ability to work together collaboratively and resolve our differences is more in keeping with our values, in alignment with who we want to be, and how we envision our relationship unfolding. The power of Olivier reminding me of his commitment to stay in relationship also reaffirms for me that he's fully committed to taking 100% responsibility for our relationship, no matter what unfolds or how we show up. Articulating his intention to stay was truly a game changer for us.

Conversely, physically staying in a conflict and saying we are staying while refusing to be emotionally present or avoiding the situation, discussion, or conflict is a faux stay. It can take the following forms:

Stonewalling
- ♦ I don't want to talk about it now, let's talk about it later.
- ♦ I don't know what you're talking about.
- ♦ I'm here, aren't I? What else do you want?

Contempt
- ♦ You're just a walking problem-making factory.
- ♦ You're pathetic the way you always focus on problems.
- ♦ You don't know anything.

Defensiveness
- ♦ So, I guess it's my fault now?
- ♦ I guess I can't do anything right.

Criticism
- ♦ You're always on my case.
- ♦ You're never satisfied.
- ♦ You're so negative. Can't you focus on anything positive?

John Gottman, a leading relationship researcher and expert, identified these destructive relationship behaviors as the four horsemen of the apocalypse. True staying requires we be emotionally present, curious about the person we're in relationship with, approach them with an open heart, and be willing to go into our discomfort zone. Ultimately, staying requires that we be physically and emotionally present or make a commitment to take space in order to come back and do so. Staying is a crucial step for our relationships' successes since it's impossible to hold onto a relationship if we're absent.

Our Default Conflict Responses Influence Our Ability to Stay

It's at the point between stimulus and response that the lizard part of our brain often takes over, causing us to react by fighting over the situation and its content (whether the request is reasonable, who's fault something is, etc.) or fleeing the scene. Staying requires that we have an awareness of our own default responses to conflict and those of our partner. My default response, for example, is to stay and hash it out whereas Matt is like the roadrunner – the minute conflict pops up, his first instinct is to run, leaving a cloud of dust in his wake. If we each relied on our defaults when conflicts arose, we'd likely never resolve any of them. It would also exacerbate their impacts and undermine our relationship and our ability to achieve long-term success. Instead, we've had to carefully acknowledge our own and each other's inclinations and work towards meeting each other in the middle to collaborate.

In fact, when Matt and I first decided to do the Co-Active™ Leadership program's project together, we did so partially to use it as a testing ground to see how well we could collaborate. As the time approached, however, I noticed Matt's certainty was starting to wane. Each time we talked about working together he said yes while cutting the conversations short and avoiding my eyes. Although Matt was saying yes with his words, his body language was sending a different message. Given my strong value of integrity, I knew I wouldn't be able to work with him in the short term or on an ongoing basis if this non-verbal doublespeak was going to continue.

Since my natural inclination for dealing with conflict is to face it head on, I first tried confronting Matt directly about his conflicting messages. I was promptly met with avoidance as he said, while walking away, "Nothing's going on. Of course, I want to work together. It's going to be a great opportunity." After several attempts with similar results, I realized Matt wasn't comfortable with conflict and I was going to have to take a white glove approach. And so, throughout the week, I asked him pointed questions, leaving lots of space for whatever might emerge, hoping for the outcome I wanted without being attached to it. Our conversations took place in short spurts, allowing both of us to hear what the other person had to say, explore it together, and reflect on what was said.

As Matt aired his fears, we were able to delve into them together. The more honest he was with me, the more I aired my own concerns. Through this process, we were able to drop our defenses and share what our marriages meant to us, our longings for the future, different possibilities we could envision, and our feelings around them. In the end, we agreed to fully commit to working together on the project while staying open to emerging possibilities without committing to anything in the future until it felt right for both of us. By staying in relationship with one another, despite our discomfort, by keeping our hearts open, and by displaying vulnerability to one another without armoring up, we were able to navigate our conflict, better understand each another, and find a third way of moving forward that circumvented the need to decide forevermore between working together or not.

Staying also requires having an awareness of any default responses to conflict our relationship may have created over the long run. If one of us, for example, has an aversion to conflict and is likely to flee at the very thought of engaging in it, both of us may have made an unconscious or conscious choice to avoid conflict by whatever means necessary, thereby creating a long-term pattern of avoidance. While this may work for a time, this pattern can lead to a buildup of issues creating a subtle undercurrent that pulls both of us away from one another or an obvious tsunami of resentment and conflict that can seem insurmountable and makes it appear harder to stay. Staying in relationship as we change these default patterns can make all the difference in terms of positive outcomes and our overall relationship satisfaction.

Knowing When to Stay and When to Go

We sometimes find ourselves in situations with people where staying feels very difficult. In families, in marriages, and in work environments, we don't always have the luxury of simply leaving. In relationships involving family ties as well as in work environments involving economic and career ties, choosing to leave can come at a great cost to us. As can staying.

It's important to remember we always have a choice, even when it doesn't seem as if we do. When our relationship's boundary (values and stay) is cracked and/or trespassed on too many times, division, resentment, politics, abrasiveness, abuse, and unhealthy conflict are invited in. Staying is a choice and it may not be our ideal one. Having an awareness of our values and how we're oriented within our relationship and in relation to our partner can help us choose to stay or leave our relationship.

Sometimes, we may choose to stay in our relationship with our hearts at a distance from our partner's but not truly overlapping. This more superficial type of relationship may serve us, our partner, and our relationship for a period, or it may serve us indefinitely, allowing our relationship to shift and grow, ultimately taking a new form. What's most important is, if we stay within our relationship's boundary, our hearts can move closer together or further apart while always being in relation with one another.

As a single mom, for many years, Josh and I were extremely close, often able to read each other's minds and anticipate what the other would do next. Our hearts were always together and overlapping since we spent most of our free time together, perfectly in alignment as to which activities we'd do, the type of music we'd listen to, the movies we enjoyed, and the humor we shared.

Josh is now a teenager who's fifteen going on twenty-seven. As he entered his tween years and developed interests separate from mine, musical tastes I couldn't relate to, and humor that was beyond me, I noticed a space insert itself between us, one that's sometimes filled with conflict and sometimes filled with abundant love. While I always love Josh beyond measure, our hearts began to drift in an awkward dance of approach and avoidance, much like the indecisive shuffle of twelve-year-old boys and girls at their first dance.

This dance of hearts overlapping and hearts apart has gone on for several years now and serves us both in different ways. The space between allows each of us to begin fumbling our way into new ways of being with each other as he approaches adulthood and independence, find our own paths as we disentangle from one another, and find room to create and grow into the new relationship that's slowly emerging. At the same time, our love for each other, the boundary of our mother and son relationship, and our shared values, help reinforce our connection while reminding us we have time and space to morph into a new incarnation that serves both of us as we develop and expand.

Other times, we may choose to stay open to being in relationship but leave our relationship's current parameters. In these cases, leaving our relationship's current container can sever our relationship in the short term with the potential of serving it over the long run. Separating, taking space, leaving our relationship for a while and focusing on other aspects of our professional and personal lives can be beneficial. Doing this involves letting the other person know our current relationship is no longer serving us, that we're moving to a new map with a new geography, and that, if they so choose, they can move onto the new map with us where we can co-design our relationship's new terms, boundaries, and landscape.

My family, for example, has a long history of loose if not non-existent boundaries. Growing up, I was accustomed to this and never thought much about it, taking the intrusions, unsolicited advice and instructions, and invasion of my personal space and possessions as par for the course, perceiving it as just part of being in a family. As I moved into adulthood, I found it not only manageable but a desired norm.

Recently, though, something in me changed and I discovered I was no longer able to tolerate the loose boundaries characterizing my familial relationships and the chronic overstepping occurring in my household. As I laid out new, clearer boundaries with my parents, I was met with resistance, criticism, and pushback. True to systems theory, as I attempted to change our relationship, my parents pushed back, and tension escalated until the system broke.

Although I'm no longer willing to stay and play within our previously existing landscape, I'm still staying open to being in a relationship with my parents. I've stepped off our existing map and moved on to a new one into which I'm inviting them. While we've yet to determine our relationship's new boundaries and landscape following our relationship rupture, I'm taking full responsibility for holding space for re-establishing our relationship in a new map so our hearts can once again come together.

Even if we choose to leave a conflict and our relationship, there's always a chance we may return. This chance is increasingly likely if the other person stays, holding the relationship while creating space for us to come back. If the other person also leaves, it's harder for either of us to come back to the relationship because there's nothing visible to come back to. It's also not impossible. Even if both of us leave our relationship, there's always a chance we can come together and reconnect.

My friend Rebecca and I have known each other almost since the day I was born. We grew up in the same house from the age of three until I was eleven. Rebecca and her twin sister lived with their parents on the top flat of our duplex while my brother and I lived downstairs with our parents. The basement was a common area for all of us kids, the zone where imagination and creativity met differences and territorial fights. Essentially, we grew up like sisters, taking sides against each other when embroiled in disagreements, and having each other's backs when others were involved.

After my parents split up and our family moved across town, our friendship was sporadic through some of our teenage years, but we reconnected as we entered our twenties. At that time, we were both finding our feet, moving into adulthood, with Rebecca three years ahead of me on this journey. As we found a new dance to our relationship, some of the same childhood patterns carried through: our familiar dynamic of older, more worldly and desirable sister and tag-along younger sister who wanted attention and to be included persisted.

Over the years, as we each got married, had children, and I got divorced from my first husband, this dynamic became more accentuated. When Rebecca got divorced years later, knowing she was struggling, I called and texted frequently throughout the process and listened for as long as she needed when she called. As time went on, our relationship became predominantly about Rebecca's needs and, feeling like there wasn't any space for mine, I hurt. When I tried to talk to her about how I felt, I was met with defensiveness and finger-pointing. After a while, I put this issue on the backburner.

One summer, when I realized I'd be going to a week-long training session near Rebecca's home, we decided I'd visit with her beforehand. Although I was really looking forward to it, as the date approached, I noticed I was becoming more and more uncomfortable with the idea of visiting Rebecca and didn't know how to tell her or even how to initiate the conversation in a way she'd be open to. The more awareness I had around my discomfort, the more I descended into it, becoming almost paralyzed. Eventually, I decided not to go see Rebecca and, acting completely outside my value of integrity, did nothing. I didn't call and tell her, and I didn't answer any of her calls or texts. For all intents and purposes, I engaged in very aggressive and divisive behavior by ghosting her.

Once Rebecca realized what was going on, she called me several times, leaving messages acknowledging and apologizing for her behavior over the past while. At this point, I was too overwhelmed with everything that had built up between us and didn't answer. In the end, Rebecca sent me a text that said, "Hi Tanya. I never heard back from you so I'm assuming you don't want us to see each other when you're in the Bay Area. I had left my weekend open, but I'll make other plans if you don't want to be in contact. I'm really sad you've decided to cut me off after being friends for 46 years. The door is still open on my end if you can be open to repair. Take good care of yourself and your family. Love, Rebecca."

Knowing Rebecca was staying in and holding our relationship for us without a time limit, I took time to process my feelings and figure out what I wanted to do next. Having the space to do this, knowing that whatever we chose to do next was up to us both, I took seven months to figure out what was truly in my heart, what I wanted to explore, and where I was hoping we'd go. Eventually, I sent her a text saying, "Hi Rebecca, I've been thinking about you a lot lately. I'm sorry I stopped communicating with you – I know it was hurtful and I'm sorry. If you're still open to talking, I'm ready to talk. Love Tanya."

Rebecca appreciated my message and let me know she was still open to talking. By staying in relationship with me without being attached to a specific outcome (ending or maintaining it), Rebecca created space for our relationship to continue even though I'd left. As a result, we were able to have a conversation in which we openly shared our hearts' truths about our experience of our relationship and each other's expectations, our perceptions and feelings, including our fears, hurts, and areas of vulnerability, and our desires for our relationship moving forward. In the end, we decided to continue developing our friendship. Rebecca committed to checking in with me to see how I'm doing on a more regular basis and supporting me when I need it, and I committed to talking with Rebecca if I became frustrated well before I felt the need to turn away.

As time went on, our relationship evolved into a stronger and more balanced one. Old dynamics and patterns dropped away as we became more comfortable talking about what was important to us and sharing our expectations, knowing we were both committed to staying, no matter what showed up.

Eventually, both of us started to feel equally loved and supported by the other. By staying, Rebecca created conditions that allowed our hearts to move closer together and for a new, healthier relationship to emerge.

How Will We Benefit from Choosing to Stay?

Leaving a difficult situation or relationship completely means our conflict has a low probability of resolving itself and that our relationship also has a low probability of repairing itself and becoming stronger. Leaving also means our relationship will no longer have the potential to be of value to us or the other person or be inspiring in any way. Instead, it will probably plateau or spiral downwards.

Staying in the pause, in our situation, and in our relationship allows for intimacy to develop. Intimacy is the ability to see into another person's heart with veils lifted and armor put aside. It happens when we maintain eye contact, exchange our hearts' truths, respect each other's values, provide physical contact, stay connected, share our fears, and willingly expose our vulnerabilities to one another. In an intimate or personal relationship, it may look like openly admitting we're scared about losing our relationship and that we feel distant from the other person. Or, it may take the form of asking for more help while admitting we can no longer carry our current load. In a corporate environment, it may be as simple as a leader admitting they got lost and don't know what the next step is, or a heartfelt apology for a mistake made.

In both business and personal relationships, staying may involve sharing our truth and courageously asking for help. Doing so allows us to recover to one another (return to ourself and one another and find our source of connection) while building our sense of trust and safety, both of which build intimacy. Intimacy builds synergy and creates an upwards spiral we can ride with our partners into self-expression, confidence, and unity. This, in turn, allows us to shift from fear to courageous connection and a knowing that we can recover to each other in times of stress. Recovering to each other also builds resiliency. Each recovery we make while staying in relationship strengthens our sense of intimacy, safety, and trust. Ultimately, personal and organizational results, success, and resiliency occur at the speed of trust which is based on the strength of our commitment to stay.

Our relationship as a unique entity also strengthens through this process of stay and recover, so it becomes more powerful, wise, creative, generative, and resourceful than the individuals in it. Performance and results emanating from this type of relationship contribute towards mutual success and full self-expression. Ultimately, being seen, heard, and known by another inside a solid container allows our hearts to approach and, eventually, overlap and align around common goals, purposes, and values so we can grow together and achieve more than we could on our own. Staying is at the heart of this and at the heart of effective leadership.

Key Points

- Stay refers to the choice to remain in relationship with ourself and with another, regardless of changes, obstacles, emotions, and conflicts encountered.

- Choosing to stay in our emotions, in our current situation, and in our relationship, even when we're uncomfortable, can build intimacy and trust.

- Understanding our natural tendencies in times of change and conflict helps us respond with intention and in alignment with our values. This improves our relationship dynamics.

- When presented with conflict, we can fight, flee, freeze, deny or ignore, accommodate, negotiate or compromise, or collaborate. Only collaboration has the potential to create positive and lasting change.

- Choosing to stay while engaging in stonewalling, contempt, defensiveness, or criticism are damaging and ineffective for our relationship and for generating positive outcomes.

- Staying is not a mandate. Strengthening our ability to discern when to stay, how to recover, when to leave, and/or when to return, improves our relationships and leadership effectiveness.

- Leaving a relationship can reset our landscape and shift conditions, ultimately providing us with an entryway to return and be in an improved relationship or a new one.

Putting Concepts into Practice

Practice #1

Download the HTI Conflict-o-meter (www.htiinstitute.com/resources). Think about your family dynamics. What were you taught about conflict? Circle the area on the meter that best represents your current relationship with conflict. Journal about what you circled. What are you aware of now? If you could move the needle, where would you move it to and what would be the impact on your relationships? What are three steps you can take to turn the dial towards your desired state?

Practice #2

Journal. How you currently engage in (or avoid) conflict has costs and benefits associated with it. Describe your behavior when you're in or avoiding conflict. List three advantages and three disadvantages this style offers you. List three benefits and three disadvantages this style has for the person(s) you're in conflict with. How does your approach to conflict strengthen your relationship? How does it weaken it?

Practice #3

Think of a relationship that causes you stress and yet you cannot avoid. This may be with a co-worker, your manager, or even a family member. Without putting yourself in danger, choose to stay in their presence for longer than normal. As you stay, what do you notice about yourself? What do you physically feel? How do you feel emotionally? If your feelings could talk, what would they say? Write down what you would say if you could say anything you want to the other person.

Knowing WIIFW (what's in it for we) and keeping it front and center in our relationships is key to achieving long-term success and satisfaction for us personally, for our relationships, and for our shared purpose and mission.

CHAPTER FIVE

The Relationship Stake

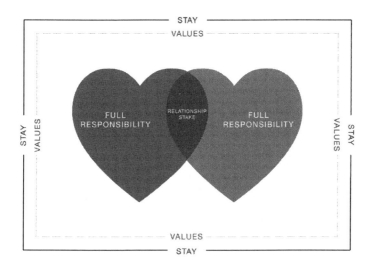

Many of us are taught at a young age that it's a dog-eat-dog world. And, this message is reinforced as we progress through life. "There's no room for everyone at the top. Only one person can be number one. You eat what you kill. You need to be better than your competitors. Doing more than

your fair share means you're being taken advantage of."
Consequently, most of us have become proficient at figuring
out what's in it for me (WIIFM) to survive and thrive.

Being good at figuring out WIIFM can get us far in life,
helping us rise through the ranks and achieve wealth,
credentials, and accolades for our various accomplishments.
Unfortunately, being good at figuring out WIIFM doesn't
work so well in relationships, especially when attaining
WIIFM comes at the other person's expense or at the
expense of collaboration, co-creation, and intimacy. In fact,
paying attention to WIIFM at the expense of paying
attention to what's in it for you (WIIFY) or what's in it for
we (WIIFW) is often an indication that a relationship is
coming to its end.

While most of us are highly skilled at thinking about our
own interests and how to achieve them and somewhat
skilled in thinking about what others need, rarely do we
think about our relationships as entities that have their own
needs to survive and thrive. These needs form the basis for
determining WIIFW and figuring this out isn't so obvious.
It requires knowing what's in it for us, what's in it for the
people we're in relationship with and being able to identify
the intersection between the two.

Identifying this intersection lets us tie various concepts
together: knowing our own and our partners' values, what
motivates us, what drives us, and what fulfills us. These may
be consistent over time or be distinct for a specific time and
place. Once we've identified what we both need and what
our relationship needs, we can determine WIIFW for the
long haul and for specific instances or events. Knowing
WIIFW and keeping this front and center in our
relationships is key to achieving long-term success and
satisfaction for us personally, for our relationship, and for

our shared purpose and mission. Having a relationship stake[4] helps us do this.

What Is a Relationship Stake?

A relationship stake is like a pole we plant in the ground. It's a joint claim we make for specific situations in our lives that lets us know what we need to hold up above all else, regardless of what shows up. It determines what we're willing to go to the mat for and reminds us about what we're in service of. Placing a relationship stake front and center helps us solidify the sentiment and theme of how we want to be in relationship together. Each decision we make that supports our relationship stake strengthens our relationship and brings our hearts closer together.

A relationship stake isn't a goal or an outcome we're trying to achieve. Instead, it informs our shared purpose and helps us determine the impact we want to have on ourself, each other, our relationship, the situation we find ourselves in, and those around us. It also helps us stay focused on our higher purpose.

Some examples of relationship stakes Matt and I have used at different points include:

♦ This relationship is important, and we are open to possibilities

♦ Fun and focus

♦ Our relationship is more important than the business

---

4. Henry Kimsey-House developed the concept of a Leadership Stake. The HTI relationship stake was built on this concept. To learn more about a Leadership Stake, read "What's Your Stake" at https://coactive.com/blog/. whats-your-stake/.

- Fun, learn, and grow
- Awesome massive value
- Orange you ready for connection, community, and collaboration?

Relationship stakes are sometimes literal and easy to understand. Other times they're somewhat elusive, only having meaning to those who create them. They often become a shorthand for a backstory to which everyone in the relationship agrees. For example, in *Orange you ready for connection, community, and collaboration,* for us, orange represents an overwhelming desire and feeling of can-do excitement and engagement. We used this stake in a team meeting where people entered disconnected, working against each other, and feeling hopeless about their ability to be impactful. By the end of the meeting, the group's attitude changed: perceiving they were working together towards a common goal, people were now eager to work together and share information and felt they could accomplish the goal in the set time frame. Energy was high and the group left looking forward to getting started and engaging with one another.

The following elements define relationship stakes.

Co-Created

Because a relationship stake informs and helps identify actions supporting and taking away from our relationship, one person cannot create it in isolation or impose it on another. Creating a relationship stake that incorporates what's important to you, me, and we requires everyone be involved in the creation process.

This process of co-creation may take some time, multiple conversations, and several iterations and is essential for the resulting relationship stake to have equal meaning for everyone. Rushing the process risks resulting in a compromised relationship stake that's lopsided in terms of overly or entirely representing one person's values, vision, and desires.

Without a common meaning and value, it's hard for each person to voluntarily choose a relationship stake and claim it repeatedly over time. Lack of common meaning and value also increases the risk that when we make decisions in times of conflict or crisis, we won't make them in alignment with our relationship stake. As fallible humans, we often allow convenience and self-interest to take precedence in these moments. A co-created relationship stake increases the likelihood that we'll make the *right* decisions, versus comfortable or convenient ones, in times of ease and difficulty. This, in turn, increases the probability that our relationship will have long-term success and we'll reach our and our relationship's desired outcomes.

While our relationship stake can change over time, its importance never changes. If we change it, we must change it together. Everyone in our relationship needs to agree on the change and it must be equally meaningful for all of us. Failing to do this puts our relationship stake at risk and diminishes its power. A team in a work environment, for example, may have a different relationship stake, depending on its development stage. A forming team may have a relationship stake of *acceptance, openness, and non-judgment* whereas a team in the performing stage may have a relationship stake of *synergy, creativity, and precision.* Similarly, a team working on a project may have a different relationship stake for each project phase. To be effective, however, each team member needs to be involved in creating the new relationship stake and agree on its final form. Leaving anyone out of this process or failing to get their agreement risks compromising the relationship stake's integrity and its ability to stand strong or be of service when conflict or problems arise.

Time or Event Bound

A relationship stake exists for a specific amount of time. It has a beginning and an end and doesn't last forever. It can exist for an hour, a day, a year, or a period of time or event agreed upon by everyone involved (for example, a team meeting, a family holiday or gathering, a family trip, a party, a product development cycle, or an offsite event).

When Olivier and I married a few years ago, we had a relationship stake of *intimacy above all* for our wedding. This stake informed every decision we made around this event, including:

- *Where we were going to get married* – at a friend's parents' house on the water.
- *Who we invited* – only friends and family in our inner circle with whom we had meaningful and long-standing relationships.
- *How many people we invited* – no more than we could each have a real conversation with over the course of the event.
- *How we prepared for the event* – Olivier designed and built the chuppah under which we were married, and close friends and I spent days setting up indoor and outdoor spaces as we cooked, collected flowers and seashells for table centerpieces, and relaxed together.
- *The event's flow* – people came early to mingle with one another in the afternoon sun so they could get to know

one another while lounging on the sun-drenched patio, by the water, or next to a cheese bar supplied by a friend. Next, an intimate ceremony where our marriage contract, designed and painted by my mother, was read aloud to include our guests, followed by hora dancing composed of intertwining rings of human connection and a buffet dinner where people could mingle and connect. The evening ended with ocean swimming, dancing, and dessert as guests reclined on couches and the night's community came together.

Our relationship stake of *intimacy above all* also informed how we showed up towards one another and towards others during this period. Olivier's mother, two sisters, and four nieces and nephews arrived two weeks before our wedding to stay with us. They live across the country and it was their first time visiting. By the time my brother, sister-in-law, and childhood friend showed up, our 2,000 square foot home was feeling cramped as family tensions, unresolved issues, and wedding jitters surfaced.

Remembering our relationship stake of *intimacy above all* and constantly reminding each other of it, including the fact that intimacy doesn't always look pretty or run smoothly, helped Olivier and me manage our emotions more gracefully than we otherwise would have. This allowed us to appreciate everyone, including the time, energy, and money they expended to support us as we formalized our commitment to one another. In the end, our relationship stake helped us create not just a day filled with love, laughter, and connection, where forty-five mostly strangers left connected as friends, but an unprecedented experience of familial connection and intimacy in the period around the actual event.

Non-Exclusive

Relationship stakes are non-exclusive. We can have multiple relationship stakes in effect at the same time. We can create multiple stakes with a person we're in relationship with, each one for a different period or event. At the same time, we can have relationship stakes with other people we're in relationship with. We may simultaneously have specific and unique relationship stakes with our partner, our manager, our parents, our team or business partner, our religious community, etc.

Four months before Olivier and I got married, Josh had his bar mitzvah. Given how closely both events took place, planning for both overlapped. The relationship stake Olivier and I developed for Josh's bar mitzvah, *important life milestones need to be celebrated and witnessed,* was very different from our wedding's relationship stake of *intimacy above all.* Needless to say, Josh's bar mitzvah was much larger than our wedding, filled with current and long-term friends and family, all of whom came from near and far to witness and celebrate this milestone with us in a more lavish and solemn setting.

Similarly, when Matt and I formalized our business relationship, we created a relationship stake of *the relationship is more important than the business.* This relationship stake informs all our interactions and business decisions and is a place we recover to when one of us isn't meeting the other's expectations. For example, when I was deciding how to approach Matt about an imbalance in our work loads, I was worried about how he would respond. I also knew that if the imbalance continued it would harm our relationship and business, and so turned to our stake for help. When I finally raised the issue, Matt, in turn, turned to our stake. Instead of becoming defensive, he reminded himself that I wouldn't be raising the issue if it wasn't important to our relationship and, instead, responded with curiosity. Matt and I also have other relationship stakes for specific events, such as when we facilitate (for example, *fun, learn, and grow*), or workdays when we want to accomplish specific things (for example, *focus, energy, and creativity*).

In the same period that Matt and I created our original relationship stake, Olivier needed to visit his aging and ailing parents across the country. Knowing he was likely to be triggered by family dynamics and unresolved issues, we created a relationship stake of *connection until death* for his visit. Even though I wasn't on the trip with Olivier nor interacting with his parents, having a relationship stake for the two of us allowed me to support him in his vision of how he wanted to interact with and show up for his family. It also helped me refocus my reactions and interpretations to what he was saying, filtering them through this lens. When, for example, he was abrupt with me, I was able to see it as an outflow of his frustration resulting from being cooped up with his parents for four days while having the same conversation over and over again as he made an effort to stay present and connected. This understanding helped me not react to his tone and, instead, give him space to talk about his feelings and concerns until he was ready to re-engage and reconnect with his parents with an open heart. Ultimately, having this relationship stake allowed Olivier to move beyond his immediate irritations and create connection and memories that he could take away from his visit for the future.

Provides a Lens

A relationship stake provides context, not content. It's a guiding sentiment or theme, not a concrete achievement with rules and regulations. It helps us determine how we'll do things; it doesn't tell us what to do. At the end of the day, it's the spirit of the law, not the letter of the law, and it provides us with a guiding impetus for determining what's important and what's not.

A relationship stake doesn't tell us what to look at. Instead, it shapes and colors how we look at things, how we think about them, and how we process information. It provides us with a lens we can look through, a filter we can interpret events through, and a screen through which we can communicate.

Having a relationship stake helps us not take things personally. It depersonalizes our experience and, ultimately, provides us and our partners with an orientation point we can hold on to as we proceed. It also pulls us back to what's important when we find ourselves adrift.

Recently, Olivier, Josh, and I went on a family vacation to Australia. Since this is my second marriage and Olivier came to parenting at a late stage, traveling together as a family is still new for us and we sometimes erupt into conflict around differing expectations and needs. After talking about our expectations, needs, and desires around the upcoming trip, Olivier and I created a relationship stake for ourselves of *family, fun, and togetherness.* What this doesn't mean is that we always needed to stay glued to the hip or every moment be orchestrated for maximum pleasure and enjoyment. Instead, this relationship stake provided us with a lens through we could make decisions as we moved forward through our holiday.

For example, it helped us answer the following questions with the aim of bringing us more in alignment with our relationship stake:

- Is this pre-scheduled activity that was supposed to be fun delivering what was intended now that we're here and tired? If not, how do we want to handle the situation?
- Will time spent apart during the holiday create distance or togetherness? Is togetherness physical or emotional?
- How do we want to handle conflict to stay in alignment with *family, fun, and togetherness*? Is conflict part of being together as a family?

Having this relationship stake allowed us to interpret unfolding events through its lens and make decisions that served us and our relationship as opposed to ones that may have fallen in line with one or more person's expectations but didn't further us towards who we want to be and how we want to be in relationship with one another.

Possible and Attainable

Because a relationship stake isn't unidimensional, black and white, a goal, or an outcome, achieving and living into it can take many forms. It reflects our purpose, a purpose that's rooted in our own, our partner's, and our relationship's values. A relationship stake is something that's possible and attainable even though its success isn't always objectively measurable. We know our relationship stake is alive and in effect when we feel we're in alignment with our values, our purpose, and the backstory we've set through our relationship stake.

Bringing a relationship stake to life doesn't involve judgment, personal attachment to being right or wrong, winning or losing, or keeping score. Instead, it requires:

- Openness towards and acceptance of our differences;
- Curiosity;

- Accepting our current state as our starting point;
- Being open to different and multiple perspectives;
- Tapping into and expressing what's in our hearts and on our minds.

When we do this, we bring our relationship stake to life and honor its importance. We know we've done this because we, our partners, and our relationship feel in alignment and on purpose.

Why Is a Relationship Stake So Important?

A relationship stake isn't a convenience or a nice to have. Instead, it's an essential: what we hold above all else. Without it, we and our partners may become susceptible to momentary whims, self-interests, or the path of least resistance. While this may be pleasurable and bring us joy in the short term, it may negatively impact us, our partners, and our relationship's health over the long term.

Since our relationship stake is unwavering and remains in effect for the period of time that we design, regardless of outcome or achievement, its indisputable power allows us to develop a commitment to what is (not what we think should be) and an openness to possibilities. Our relationship stake serves as a unifying bond enabling us to stay rooted in our values and recover (return to ourself and one another, and find our source of connection) when things go awry.

Because our relationship stake is heart-centered and heart-generated, it's multifaceted, includes shades, and is flexible enough to be expressed in multiple ways. This allows our egos to take a back seat in our decision-making process and helps us manage problems and conflict from our hearts, not just our heads. Its permission-granting nature also empowers us to try new ways of being and acting in our efforts to reach and maintain alignment with our purpose and each other.

Just as adding guy lines to anchor a pole in the ground allows the pole to stand strong, regardless of its environment, making decisions that support our relationship stake allows it to remain firmly planted at our relationship's center so it can support us as we navigate our way, together. Although some of our decisions may undermine our relationship stake or fail to support it, recovering to our relationship stake allows it and our relationship to persevere, grow, and endure.

Key Points

- What's in it for me (WIIFM), what's in it for you (WIIFY), and what's in it for we (WIIFW) are three great distinctions that simultaneously honor our natural survival instincts and our mutual desire for connection.

- A relationship stake is found in the intersection between WIIFM, WIIFY, and WIIFW.

- A relationship stake isn't a goal or an outcome. It informs our shared purpose and helps elevate our focus to a higher common good.

- Relationship stakes are co-created, time bound, non-exclusive, possible, and attainable.

- Relationship stakes provide us with a lens through which we can interpret events, information, and communicate.

- Relationship stakes keep us in alignment with our values and purpose and provide a means through which we can recover in times of conflict or misalignment.

Putting Concepts into Practice

Practice #1

Journal. Think about the last time you traveled somewhere with a friend, family member, or co-worker. What were two positive and two negative memories as they relate to your relationship on this trip? If you could go back in time and create a relationship stake before the trip, what relationship stake would you create? What impact would this stake have had on your trip? On your relationship?

Practice #2

Think of an upcoming event taking place in the next thirty days (for example, a birthday, a business meeting, a day trip, or even just a short visit/lunch with a person in your life). You have the power to influence your time together. Describe how you intend for this time-bound interaction to go. If it was a color, what color would you paint the scene? If theme music accompanied you, describe its genre, volume, and characteristics. What energy do you hope is in the space around and in you? Describe the feelings in the atmosphere around you.

With all of this in mind, write down the relationship stake you'd like to create. (Note: Relationship stakes are co-created. Practicing on your own is a great place to start, and we suggest inviting those with whom you'll attend the event into co-creating the stake with you.)

Infinite options and perspectives are available to us. Having options and a process to navigate changes in our situation ensures we're more likely to respond to change with intentionality, reaching our mutually desired destination, together.

CHAPTER SIX

Stop, Think, Choose, Implement (STCI)

No matter how carefully we focus on our purposes, values, goals, and plans, we'll encounter unexpected triumphs and tragedies. As we try to move towards our desired state, we can sometimes derail ourselves. We make mistakes, doubt creeps in, and a lack of confidence and discipline can alter our chosen path. Changing conditions, unexpected events, and the dynamics of our relationships can also wreak havoc with our plans or bring us unexpected successes, changing our life's momentum and direction.

Being aware of ourself, our environment, and our relationships gives us the opportunity to adapt and intentionally make proactive changes. STCI (pronounced "sticky") is a tool that can help us do this. Before we can use the SCTI tool, however, we need to develop an awareness of our situational and relationships' environments.

Awareness

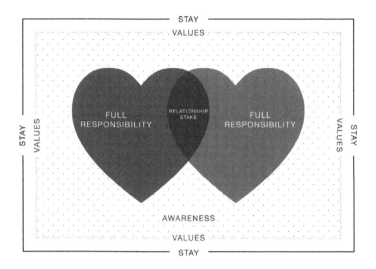

Being aware of what's going on in our environment helps us address subtle shifts happening within us and around us in a timely manner. Environmental awareness also helps us determine which adjustments we need to make to get to our desired destination and whether we need to adjust our destination.

Being aware involves being attuned to what's in our atmosphere and using all our senses, intuition, and instincts to notice what's going on around us and identify our and our environment's overriding feeling and state. While it's easier to identify concrete changes in our environment (for example, weather, traffic flow, and neighborhood density), emotional and relationship atmospheric changes are less tangible yet equally important for us to identify.

Each of our relationships has its own complex atmosphere that changes over time. These atmospheres contain a variety of elements, such as:

- context
- content
- tension/pressure
- perspectives
- mind over heart or vice-versa
- feelings (for example, love, rage, warmth, etc.)
- temperature/energetic charges (for example, positive, neutral, negative, synergy, lethargy, toxicity, etc.)

Whatever we're contributing to our relationship through our actions, behaviors, thoughts, and emotions affects our relationships' atmospheres.

In cosmological terms, an environmental atmosphere is a layer of gases surrounding a planet, held in place by the planet's gravity. In relational atmospheres, gravity is a combination of what pulls us together, what pulls us apart, and what each of us is willing to pull into our relationship. It's our commitment to one another and to our relationship. If we aren't committed to staying, we generally don't have a high degree of gravitational pull towards one another. We can easily disengage or flee from our relationship when its atmosphere becomes unstable or charged.

On the opposite end of the spectrum, when our relationships have too much gravity or closeness, it often shows up as neediness and imbalanced demands: one of us crowds the other person's space or micromanages them. We find it hard to breathe, feel suffocated and controlled, and perceive that there's little room for either of us to move. As our relationship moves in this direction, our independence, identity, or the relationship itself becomes threatened.

We can always change our relationship's atmosphere; we only need to desire change and decide to put in the required effort. Without making this choice, whatever is currently present in our relationship's atmosphere is likely to remain and, possibly, amplify over time. Toxicity often breeds toxicity, for example, whereas positivity typically breeds more positivity.

Because our hearts aren't always overlapping with one another and because our relationship stake doesn't always knit us together, developing a constant awareness of the atmosphere that exists in relation to our partner helps us gauge our relationship. Are we hearts apart and still in positive relationship, using the space between us to expand and grow so we can come back together stronger? Or, are we hearts apart with growing divisiveness and animosity, ultimately weakening our relationship? Developing an awareness of what's emerging, the direction our relationship is flowing in, and what's true for us, the other person, and our relationship helps us determine whether we want to take responsibility and adjust our direction and stay the course or not. Once we've established that we've chosen to stay and work on aligning our hearts, slowing down and using the STCI process as a navigational tool is a simple and effective way to transform our relational atmosphere and effect change. Let's look at STCI now.

STCI

I was working on developing a Violence Prevention program for British Columbia's healthcare workers. Stakeholders included consultants and representatives from all six provincial health authorities, the provincial workplace safety organization, unions, and the organization responsible for safety in healthcare. Timelines were tight – we had to develop five online courses in seven months – and consensus was required to establish all course objectives and content. Two months in, competing needs, different perspectives, politics, and lack of available stakeholder time were slowing the process. That's when my phone rang.

"Hi, Tanya, it's Sergio, the executive director. I'm calling to check in to see how the Violence Prevention project's going."

"It's going well. We're pretty much on track. I'm a bit worried about subject matter expert response times and some team dynamics I'm observing, but this isn't any different from any other project I've led. I'm confident we'll pass through this stage and things will start to move more quickly."

"The reason I'm calling is because even though we planned on creating the next five courses during the next fiscal year, we won't have the money. If we're going to do it, we need to do it this fiscal year. I'm wondering whether you think this is doable?"

I stopped and thought about all the variables at play, and told him, "It'll be tight, and I think it's doable. The concerns I have mostly involve response times. I know a lot of people on this project are doing it off the side of their desk and it's translating into slow response times. If we could get that addressed, I think we'd be in good shape."

"Thanks for your honesty. I'm going to raise this at the next team meeting and then we'll make our decision. I'll speak with you then."

"Sounds good. Thanks for checking in with me."

The next week, Sergio explained the situation to the stakeholders sitting around the table. Once he finished, it was so quiet you could hear a pin drop. Finally, one person said, "If I understand correctly, you're asking us to double our output over the next five months? If so, I don't see how it's possible. I mean, I'm already overloaded and finding it hard to give this project my all." As she said this, others began nodding their heads in agreement.

Sergio said, "Thanks for being so honest." He then turned to the rest of the group and asked, "What else is surfacing for you?" As others began to speak up, he listened quietly to them until they finished and mirrored back to them what he had heard to make sure he'd understood it correctly. This went on for over an hour as each person had their say.

Once everyone spoke, Sergio thanked them for being upfront and invested. He then summarized everything he'd heard. He started by listing their concerns and then described their feelings about the project's importance. He concluded by reiterating that the only way the project would be funded was during the current fiscal year. If the group waited, they might have more time but no money to complete it. Finally, he asked the group, "What do you want to do?"

With this question, something in the room shifted. The same woman who originally voiced her objections said, "This project is important and it's going to make a difference for a lot of people. Having half the courses is better than having none, but it'll be most effective if people have access to all of them. I guess we'll just have to work together and figure out how to get it done." With that, the rest of the group chimed in in agreement.

"Thank you for trusting me with your concerns. I want to acknowledge all of you for how much you care and how you're invested in making this project a success. I'll let the board know we'll be moving forward with full development."

STCI is a relationship-centered methodology. It helps us slow down and create space to consciously and systematically make our next move, a move that:

+ keeps us in our relationship;

+ keeps us in alignment with our values;

+ serves our relationship stake, us, our partners, and our relationship;

♦ keeps us progressing towards our purpose and desired outcomes while keeping us in positive relation with one another.

Unwittingly, Sergio employed the STCI methodology: staying in the discomfort, leaning into stakeholders' values, **stopping** and listening when objections and concerns were voiced, and **thinking** about different options and impacts allowed Sergio and the group to **choose** a new option. The project was subsequently completed on time and within budget, and the program was **implemented** with great positive impact.

How we proceed when trying to respond to and create change is as important, if not more so, than our intentions. We can respond emotionally and reactively, or we can use our atmospheric awareness to slow down and respond with purpose. We can ignore the changes and keep going, or we can stop and check in with ourself and our partner to find out what we're noticing. Infinite options and perspectives are available to us. Having a process for navigating our changing situations and making choices means we're more likely to intentionally adapt and respond to change and reach our mutually desired destination in partnership.

STCI is an iterative process that helps us navigate our relationships' dynamic natures and variables we can and can't control. As a process, it helps us engage the person we're in relationship with to share their perspectives, generate additional options, choose, and go the important and often courageous step of implementing our choice, together. When we use STCI, we can adjust, choose, and act by redirecting ourselves and navigating the change or conflict together.

We can complete STCI on our own or in partnership. We can conduct it slowly and formally, with a lot of rigor and intensity, or we can conduct it more informally and organically. Depending on our circumstances, we can complete the process in a split second or over an extended period. Regardless of how we conduct and complete STCI, the four steps are always repeated in the sequence listed below until we've achieved true collaboration and navigated the conflict or change together. Success is defined as hearts and minds aligned and ready to move forward, together. As a process, STCI is a perpetual cycle we never stop engaging in.

Stop

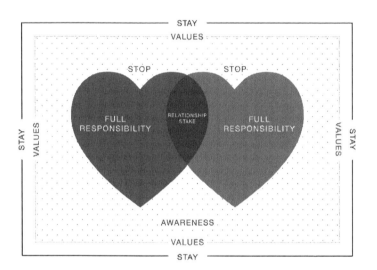

We and the people we're in relationship with are constantly changing, as is the space and atmosphere around us. Our awareness of this change is also in a constant state of flux. Some changes are overt and easy to detect, whereas others are more subtle, requiring our senses be highly attuned to pick them up.

Our body, more often than our mind, gives us the first clue that something in our atmosphere is off. We may suddenly get a feeling or a knowing that something's shifted in the space around us even if nothing's overtly changed. Some of us feel it in our gut, some of us feel it as a shift in our overall being (for example, a tightening in our chest, a tingling sensation on our skin, a sense of lightness or joy), while others experience it as a change in the emotional temperature enveloping us. As soon as we're aware that the atmosphere around us has changed, the first STCI step is to stop whatever we're doing, thinking, or saying.

Stopping is important. It prevents us from blindly reacting to the person or situation in front of us and provides us with a window for thinking about potential impacts and consequences. It allows us to slow our mind down and prevents us from reacting and saying something emotional. It also creates the time and space to travel the eighteen inches from our mind to our heart so we can hold on for a moment, hold on to our relationship stake, hold on to our relationship, hold togetherness, and simply look around and observe what we're feeling and thinking with highly attuned senses.

Initially, stopping may involve saying nothing while focusing on our body's chemical responses, observing our heart rate, breath, and temperature. If any of these are elevated, reconnecting with our breath and intentionally slowing it down (for example, doing deep belly breathing) until our heart rate and temperature lower allows us to proceed from a more centered space. Pausing helps us deepen and widen our sense of the world within and around us.

If we decide to share that we've stopped or have hit pause before moving forward, it's important to emphasize that even though we're stopping, we're not leaving: we're stopping in the short term so we can stay for the long haul. Regardless of how we stop, by stopping we remove some of our atmosphere's charge and create a safe foundation upon which we can both maneuver. Stopping allows us to acknowledge our atmosphere's change so we can connect and get curious from our heart while committing to staying in the change and moving through it, regardless of what emerges. Ultimately, the idea is to pull up the drawbridge so we don't have an escape route. We stop in our discomfort so we can move forward to a place of eventual comfort and reconnection with one another, to our relationship stake, and to our shared purpose and mission. Stopping sets the stage for us to develop a deeper awareness of what's going on while creating the space from which we can take the next step towards an intentional response.

Think

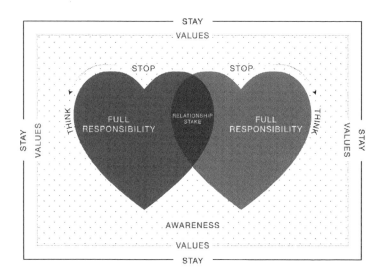

As we stop and breathe, physical, mental, and emotional space usually emerge. We can use this space to start observing what's in our atmosphere (Is it frigid, hot, tepid, distant, safe, dangerous?) and in our relationship (Are we hearts together, hearts apart, or somewhere in between?). As we identify where we are in relation to the other person, we can also observe and identify our own urges, including:

- *Feelings* – Anger, frustration, hurt, etc.
- *Reactions and actions we want to take* – Our desire to fight, flee, pretend nothing is wrong.
- *Thoughts and judgments* – He's such a jerk. She's being unreasonable. He thinks he knows everything.
- *Words we want to say* – I hate you. I'm leaving.
- *Habitual patterns that are trying to emerge* – Defensiveness/ attacking, blaming and lashing out, passive aggressiveness, retreating/stonewalling, going silent or screaming.

At the same time, we can observe what's happening with the person we're in relationship with by identifying:

- Their body language;
- The atmosphere surrounding them;
- What they're acting on and not acting on;
- Any patterns, armor, and emotional weapons they're displaying.

Simply noticing this and accepting ourself and our partner for where we're at, no matter whether we're disconnected or connected, in agreement or disagreement, may influence how we're feeling and induce a change in our atmosphere or relationship. We can do all of this as a solitary internal process or by sharing our thoughts and observations with our partner.

Once we've stopped to observe and notice what's going on for ourself, our partner, our relationship, and in our atmosphere, we're ready to process our observations and think about them. As we tune in and become aware of what's going on in and around us, we assess, interpret, and cast judgments based on what we're observing and feeling, what's happening, what we think we can control in our situation, and what our heart has to say about it. This involves thinking with our head and our heart about all our thoughts – the good, the bad, the ugly, and thoughts we're not yet fully aware of.

While there are thousands of ways we can describe what's happening around us in any given instance, we're likely to categorize it in one of the following ways:

1. A situation that's positive and adds value to our life.
2. A situation that's negative and adds value to our life.
3. A situation that's positive and subtracts value from our life.
4. A situation that's negative and subtracts value from our life.
5. A situation that's neutral in that it doesn't substantially impact our life.

Since our interpretation and categorization are unique to us, another person experiencing the same conditions in the same situation may have a different interpretation about what's going on and its impact. What's positive to us may be neutral or negative to another person and what's positive to them may be negative or neutral to us. For example, whereas Matt used to be conflict averse, perceiving any form of conflict as an automatic negative, I've always perceived conflict as something that's potentially positive. Given these differences, it's important for us to think about our current situation from different perspectives while acknowledging that infinite and equally valid perspectives exist.

Being open to our thoughts and willing to communicate and examine them with our partner or with someone else helps us find new perspectives and ward off all-knowing, black-and-white judgments that might lead us to a win/lose standoff. When I'm really upset about something, for example, I like talking with someone outside my situation or relationship. Having someone who's impartial listen to me talk about and work through my feelings helps me create space. I can then reflect on and identify the best ways to respond within the context of serving myself, the person I'm in relationship with, and our relationship. Essentially, having this external ear helps me be less reactive and creates space in which I can develop a proactive, intentional, relationship-centered response.

When we, our partner, or our relationship is experiencing atmospheric tension or a specific conflict, we can think about four main things to center ourselves:

1. The impact the current conflict is having on ourself and what outcome we want for ourself over the next week, month, year, and once the conflict has passed.

2. The impact we want to have on our partner and outcomes we want for them over the next week, month, year, and once the conflict has passed.

3. The impact we want to have on our relationship and short, medium, and long-term outcomes we're looking for as we navigate our atmospheric changes and existing conflict.

4. The impact we want to have on our relationship stake.

Thinking about these four elements provides us with a context for thinking about available options.

Possible options can include new perspectives, thoughts, specific behaviors, and actions. Identifying these involves answering the following questions:

- What options do I know about?
- What are some possible options I might not have thought of?
- Whom can I speak with to get a different perspective and shed some light on options I might not know about?

- ◆ What actions can I take that will serve my desired outcomes and our relationship stake?

- ◆ Which actions will have a negative impact on achieving my desired outcomes or on our relationship stake?

- ◆ Are there actions I can't think of and do I need to lean in and consult others to figure things out?

- ◆ Do I need to take any action at all?

Exploring these questions allows us to identify areas of disagreement, depersonalize our disagreement, think about our relationship and our context (not just the disagreement's content), and think about different options.

Thinking allows us to consider multiple perspectives and is the perfect opportunity for brainstorming. Thinking isn't choosing. Since we aren't making a choice about how we're moving forward, we can allow ourselves to play with even the most ridiculous and exaggerated options to create a laundry list of outrageous possibilities. Getting curious, being open to possibilities, and committing to what our current reality is are integral to this process.

As we think, we can do so quietly by ourselves or we can communicate with our partners so that thinking becomes the start of a connected and collaborative process in which we exchange our hearts' truths with one another. We share our heart truth feelings from a state of observation and curiosity (What I feel about this is…, What's coming up for me is…, I'm aware of this feeling inside of me….). Our heart's truth is rooted in an intuition that's deeply grounded and exists outside the dichotomies of right and wrong.

Connecting to our heart's truth, not simply to what our rational (or irrational) mind says is right or true, allows us to connect to how we feel about our situation. How we feel is how we think we feel. How we feel is our right and we're allowed to own and express it. When we're grounded in our heart's truth, we're outside judgment and analysis zones, simply delving into what's true for us in this moment. Even saying "this doesn't feel right" or "this feels wrong" creates an openness and a spaciousness that invites discussion and helps us navigate our situation with more intentionality as we explore scenarios, options, and choices.

Engaging in the think step of the STCI process helps us navigate change and increases the likelihood that we'll wind up in alignment, if not agreement, with our hearts overlapping and tethered to our relationship stake. By thinking, we start the process of exploring choices, a process that eventually leads us towards the third STCI step.

Choose

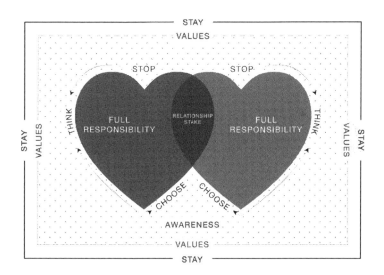

Before settling on a choice as to how we want to move forward, we often find ourselves repeatedly cycling back and forth between thinking and choosing. This is a dynamic, multidirectional part of the STCI process. The process of choosing requires we become curious about ourself and try to understand another person's feelings, perspectives, and interpretations about the same event or situation we're experiencing.

Being curious about what the person in front of us is experiencing and thinking and seeing the world through their eyes helps us identify areas of commonality. This can lead us to recognize openings where we might be in alignment. Alignment isn't agreement on outcome. Instead, it's a space occupied by a commonality of belief, commitment, and desires, and it's born out of empathy. We generate empathy the instant we begin to get curious from our hearts and the moment we take another person's perspective into consideration, treating it as a valid alternative to our own.

For many of us, entertaining a different point of view can feel like we're stacking evidence against ourself and this can be scary. Exploring someone else's perspective with curiosity to achieve understanding is not the same as agreeing with them. It's making a choice to remain committed to staying and engaging with them, even when we don't like what we're discovering or are fearful of what might lie ahead.

Exploring options and possibilities with curiosity often creates an opening where 360 degrees of potential movement can occur. As possibilities for the whole problem, part of the problem, or as something bigger emerges, we may reach agreement, continue to disagree, or continue to look for another way. Regardless of the outcome, engaging in this process ensures our hearts stay open to one another, we connect on a deeper level, and our relationship becomes stronger.

We may cycle between thinking and choosing alone or in partnership, and the process may take us seconds, minutes, days, weeks, or years. Making a choice is a process in which we distill our swirling head and heart thoughts and options into a manageable collection and repeatedly return to our relationship stake to guide us in this process. It requires identifying what we need to say yes to and what we need to say no to, to turn each specific option into a reality. Any options for which we can't or won't say yes or no to what's required aren't feasible alternatives. Simply engaging in this process and identifying actual possibilities has value in and of itself as it often brings new information to light.

Matt and I, for example, recently discussed whether he would move forward with a new opportunity that could possibly impact our business. Through our conversation, we identified potential positive and negative outcomes, including personal and professional opportunity costs (time away from business development and his family, missed revenue opportunities, costs associated with pursuing the new opportunity, conflicts of interest, intellectual property rights issues). Through this dialogue, new issues surfaced that neither of us had previously identified. By the end of our conversation, Matt was still uncertain about what his choice would be and was clearer on what he needed to focus on to make his choice.

We are usually ready to make our choice when we're centered in our heart and each of us is fully seen, fully heard, and our point of view is understood. When these criteria are met, the best option, defined as one that serves our relationship stake, our shared purpose and mission, and our relationship, while aligning with our and our partner's values, is often obvious. If an option doesn't meet these criteria, it's usually best to wait and keep exploring more ideas and potential choices to see what else is possible. We always have a choice. Always.

Since the atmosphere around us is always changing, even doing nothing is sometimes a way for us to weather a storm. Doing nothing, however, even if only for a time, is making a choice. This choice has consequences. Actively making the choice to do nothing and owning this choice changes our sense of control and influence. It changes us from feeling like a victim who's powerless to someone who is empowered and powerful.

In April 2019, a young man uttering anti-Semitic slurs while bearing an assault rifle broke into the Chabad of Poway Temple, just north of San Diego, while temple was in session for Passover. Rabbi Goldstein was in the middle of his sermon and held up his hands towards the attacker. The attacker shot at him, blowing off two of his fingers. Before he could fire a second shot, Lori Kaye, a congregant in attendance to commemorate her mother's death, protected the Rabbi by placing herself in the line of fire. Ultimately, Lori chose to save the Rabbi's life and lost her own.

Throughout, Rabbi Goldstein chose to do nothing except continue his sermon on kindness, sending the message to his congregation that they should continue to stay strong and stand together. He consciously chose to do nothing in terms of protecting himself in the face of violence and, instead of being a victim, chose to empower himself and others by insisting the Jewish values of faith, community, kindness, and love that he espoused were more powerful than any expression of hate.

Although our goal is often to bring our hearts back into alignment with one another and our relationship stake, this isn't always our best choice. Sometimes, choosing to keep our hearts at a distance from one another, or touching but not overlapping, serves us the most, providing us with time and space to grow and change until we're ready to go through the process of thinking and choosing, and make a choice together.

Ultimately, engaging in the choosing process helps us determine where we want to go when we're dislodged in our relationships. By cycling back to our relationship stake, identifying our options and values, weighing their worth to us, and re-evaluating the outcomes we're looking for, we're able to identify and choose the best course of action so we can implement it to serve us and our relationship.

Implement

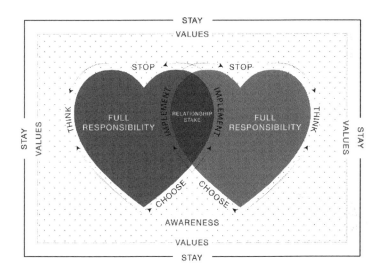

Sometimes, after thinking about which options are available to us and distilling them down to a specific choice, we don't move into the action phase. We don't implement. Although we've made a choice, fear of placing ourselves in a vulnerable position, or fear of being wrong, makes it hard for us to muster the courage to take the next step that's required for us to initiate change. We may get into a non-productive cycle of "what if" and never move into action.

However, as author Brené Brown noted in her 2019 Netflix special, courage can't exist without vulnerability and we must allow ourselves to be vulnerable to play full out in life's arena. Asking ourselves, "How is our current situation working for us? How is it working for our relationship?" can help us muster the courage to implement our choice, especially if our answers to these questions aren't positive.

Implementing our choice means we execute the thoughts, behaviors, and actions we decided on. We need to be clear on who's responsible (you, me, and/or we) for implementing each action and be clear on what our success criteria looks like. Actions may be visible, measurable, and obvious, or simply a subtle change in energy, attitude, or heart (for example, open heart, inquiry). We may need to act alone or with our partner, simultaneously, or at individual intervals and timing, to fully implement our choice.

Once we find the courage to implement our choice, we initiate a change in our atmosphere, a change we may or may not be immediately aware of. Taking action puts in motion a new series of conditions that have an impact: our actions' impact ourself, the person we're in relationship with, our relationship, and our environment.

Our next step involves evaluating the impact of our implemented choice. We can ask ourselves, alone or with our partner:

♦ How have our new thoughts, behaviors, and actions affected our relationship?
♦ Are our hearts closer together?
♦ Is our relationship stake strengthened?

♦ Did implementing our choice have our desired impact and help us move towards our desired outcomes? If so, are we fully there or only partially?

Answering these questions requires us to attune to what's in our new atmosphere and become aware of what's changed, what's the same, what our new temperature and gravitational pull is, and the impact on us, our partner, and our relationship. We may be able to answer these questions immediately after implementing our choice or it may take us hours, days, weeks, and even years before we can successfully gather the data required to answer them effectively.

Once we've taken inventory of our new set of circumstances, our next step is to determine if we want to stay in our new atmosphere. If so, we don't need to do anything except maintain awareness of our atmosphere and any developing fluctuations and changes. If we're still unhappy with our new atmosphere and our implemented choice didn't net the outcomes we and our partners are looking for, we can re-engage in the STCI process and use our awareness of our new atmosphere and related data as our new start line.

STCI in Action

I was working as the Western region's general manager for a start up in a national wireless telecommunications company. The company had spent hundreds of millions on upgrading our technology in Alberta since it was the number one province to deliver for the company. I was responsible for growing subscribers and subscriber revenue while growing our team and expanding retail points of presence. My boss was the company's VP of sales and was responsible for achieving results and meeting targets. Despite the investment in technology, our company was losing subscribers at an astronomical rate and I was failing miserably.

The worse things got, the more my boss started to micromanage me, constantly asking me, "Why did we miss targets again this week? What's going on with you and your team? Who's not performing at the rate we need them to? Why don't we have our new retail location up and running like we planned?" To make matters worse, I didn't trust Paul and Ted, the two provincial account managers who reported to me and on whom I was dependent to achieve results. The more my boss micromanaged me, the more I grew fearful, and the more I asked Paul and Ted, "What are you doing? How come? How can this possibly be what you did this week?" My tone was one of exasperation and frustration, with an underlying WTF, and my attitude was "this sucks," as I unsuccessfully tried to mask it with questions and micromanaging.

This pattern of me creating more pressure and mis-alignment due to my fear went on for two and a half months, almost a full quarter, at which point I realized I had to stop. It wasn't fun for me and it wasn't fun for Paul or Ted. I had managed to drive a wedge between us that was creating so much toxicity that I couldn't access any of their combined fifty years of experience. The atmosphere was so strained that it took all of my energy just to show up for work each day.

I realized we needed to do things differently. I thought about how I hadn't gone into the sales territory, how I'd been doing all my managing over the phone, how I wasn't really invested in the outcome, and how I'd been barking orders at everyone without consideration for them as people. As I thought about my options (go see Paul and Ted, go and visit the sales territory, or keep doing what I'd been doing), I decided to book a flight to Calgary and asked Paul and Ted to meet me for a full day's meeting at a hotel.

The three of us met for the day. I started by admitting that things were broken, that I didn't know what to do and was feeling the pressure. I suggested we make a list about what was going on. Number one on our list was we weren't having fun. Number two was my leadership was broken, and I needed help. By the end of this process, we had a list with thirty-five items on it outlining our current situation and none of it was looking pretty. As we looked head on at our list, I asked if we wanted to change the situation and the answer was a unanimous yes.

I told them we needed to be creative and come up with a new set of tactics and that I needed their help since I couldn't do it on my own. Together, we looked at each of the thirty-five items and asked ourselves what we could do to counter it. By the end of the day, we decided to own the story, let everyone in the company know we had a strategy, and that we were going to get very analytical and tactical to solve the problem.

I drove all over Alberta with my team, visiting towers that were beaming internet for communities without cable high speed internet. We talked to people on the ground and found out that although each tower was recently upgraded, at a significant cost, with high speed technology, our subscriber counts were going down because speeds weren't always as fast as we were promoting, installers were sometimes installing improperly, and towers were sometimes overloaded. We found out the sales problem was largely based on a technological issue.

As we learned more about the problem, we realized the country-wide way we'd been marketing wasn't very effective. Moving forward, we decided to market tower by tower, customizing each marketing campaign to align with the community we were targeting and accurate speeds of services we were actually providing.

At the same time, we involved others in the problem-solving process. Dealers were invited and account managers who were on the ground and lived near the towers provided market review updates to executives every two weeks. Before this, I'd always done the presentations alone. This new approach allowed for more information to surface, alignment to be created around choices to address identified problems, and implementation to occur as an integrated whole instead of in a piecemeal fashion.

As we implemented the changes using the tower by tower approach, our subscriber rates started to increase, and our company was able to gain insight into how it was operating and make new choices to improve its outcomes. Paul, Ted, and I became more effective, leaning into each other's strengths to reach our business objectives and targets, my boss was much happier, and the micromanagement stopped. In the end, stopping, thinking about our options, choosing a new approach, and implementing it together allowed us to change our atmosphere and relationship from one of toxic, fear-based claustrophobia to one characterized by trust, respect, honesty, and hard work.

Why Use STCI?

While we may be tempted to only use the STCI process when conflict or tension appears inside our relationship's atmosphere, we can also use STCI to change our relationship's atmosphere when things are going well. It can help us reinforce our current relational atmosphere by building on happiness, intimacy, and success we're already experiencing to bring it to the next level. As we consider the questions of "How great can we become together? How deep is our love and commitment to each other? What else is possible between us and for us to achieve as we journey together?", harnessing the power inherent in each step of the STCI process helps us open our relationship to unlimited possibilities.

When we're working as a team, using the STCI process surfaces issues and exposes adjustments we need to make for us to compete effectively in our chosen field of play. The same is true of organizations. No matter whether it needs to make internal adjustments or external adjustments in the marketplace, using the STCI process leverages people and teams' hearts and minds, aligning them so they can make required changes and move towards a common goal while staying tethered to their relationship stake. This is true no matter the level of change circling within an industry or in our prevailing economic climate.

Since we are never alone as we strive towards a life filled with purpose and created by design, we may find intentional living challenging as we consider other people's needs and wants. Moving forward towards a common purpose and set of goals is a complex process, one in which we usually encounter stumbling blocks. Choosing to use the STCI process to move forward in relationship with one another can reduce tension and improve collaboration, outcomes, and results. We can always use STCI. No matter what's happening around us and no matter where we're coming from or heading towards, applying STCI serves us and our relationship along the way. It works when we work it. It works simply when we work it together.

Key Points

♦ Having a sense of awareness is necessary for our survival. Awareness of the atmosphere around us and our relationships is a skill we can tune, strengthen, and use to enrich the quality of our relationships.

- All our relationships are dynamic. Being aware of what's shifting in and around us allows us to address unfolding changes.

- Combined with awareness, applying STCI (Stop, Think, Choose, Implement), together or alone, allows us to proactively address changes in our relationship and intentionally choose responses that can bring us more in alignment with our values and goals and improve outcomes.

- **Stop**: Stopping allows us to pause and check in with ourself, the other person, and our relationship, regardless of what's going on. Stopping is a powerful choice that helps keep us in relation with each other, with our relationship stake, and in alignment with our values.

- **Think**: Thinking involves using our heads and our hearts. It can be done alone or in partnership. How and what we think of any given situation is often unique to us. Expressing how we think out loud and listening to the other person's thoughts allows us to access more information, increases the number of perspectives available to use, and expands available possibilities.

- **Choose**: Making a choice involves intentionally selecting a specific option once all available options are examined. Anything to which we won't say yes and no to what's required is not a feasible choice. Looking to our relationship stake before making a choice helps ensure the choice we make is in alignment with our values, purpose, and goals.

- Cycling between thinking and choosing allows for possibilities to expand.

- **Implement**: We need to implement our choice to create a lasting change and bring about a new atmosphere. It's important to be clear on who's responsible for implementing the behaviors, actions, and thoughts for each of our choices. It's also important to be clear on what our success criteria is. We can always re-engage in the STCI process if our implemented choice doesn't obtain the results we desired.

♦ STCI is an iterative process that can happen very quickly or over a prolonged period of time. It's a process we never stop engaging in.

Putting Concepts into Practice

Practice #1

Step 1: Think about the last time you were engaged in a conflict. Write about the situation in five sentences or less.

Step 2: Write down the word STOP. Using the power of hindsight, go back in time and place yourself in the moments before the conflict sparked. How could you have hit pause and slowed down to acknowledge a conflict was brewing? Write your answer down.

Step 3: Write down the word THINK. Write about what was going on for you. Brainstorm five to eight ideas for navigating through the conflict. What are five to eight options, perspectives, or ideas for how to move forward? Write these down.

Step 4: Write down the word CHOOSE. Looking at your list of five to eight options, select an option that's different from the one you chose in the actual conflict. Why are you choosing this option and what outcomes are you hoping for?

Step 5: Write down the word IMPLEMENT. Write down one to three actions you will take based on the choice you made on how to proceed. This may include working the STCI process with the person who was also involved in the conflict or sharing your new choice with them. What do you notice about this process?

Practice #2

Download the HTI STCI Worksheet from www.htiinstitute.com/resources. Underneath each of the STCI steps, identify three or four actions you can take to bring the steps to life.

Practice #3

Think about the following questions and discuss them with someone you are in a personal or professional relationship with:

- How does using STCI benefit our relationship?
- What are the costs/disadvantages to using STCI?
- What gets in the way of you using STCI? (Both of you answer with your own barriers.)

The HTI Relationship Cornerstones are tools that help guide our hearts towards True North; the path that allows us to know where we stand, where we're aligned, and where we're heading, together.

CHAPTER SEVEN

The HTI Relationship Cornerstones

Daryl Davis, a black musician, has a knack for turning racism-based hate into friendship. Over his lifetime, he's befriended Klansmen, resulting in over 200 of them giving up their robes. It all started in his twenties when he sat down for a drink with a white man who had watched him play. As they conversed, the older man let it slip that this was the first time he'd sat down with a black man. Filled with curiosity as to how this was possible, Daryl asked him, "Why?" After hemming and hawing a bit, and a deep elbow to the side from his friend, the man finally admitted, "I'm a member of the Ku Klux Klan," and proceeded to show his Klansman membership card as proof. Despite this profound divide, Daryl and the man continued to talk, brought together by their love of music.

Daryl noticed a seed was planted and decided to nourish it. He began traveling around the country to sit down with Klansmen and talk. Over time, he committed to "what is" by accepting these white men as Klansmen while arming himself with all the knowledge about their organization and beliefs he could find. He fed his curiosity by asking them, "How can you hate me when you don't even know me?" and listening to their answers with an open heart. He spoke his heart truth as he looked for commonalities, believing that "When two enemies are talking they're not fighting... if you spend five minutes with your worst enemy you will find that you both have something in common." He also kept faith that if he worked the relationship, other possibilities would emerge. In the end, he says, "I didn't convert anybody. They saw the light and converted themselves."[5]

Relationships are a perpetual dance. A two-step requires us to harmonize our feet to achieve fluidity of movement through grace, intentional action, and coordinated movement. Similarly, relationships require that we harmonize our hearts and minds to achieve fluidity, harmony, synchronicity, and a planned agenda to create a stable foundation that can withstand shifts, changes, and growth.

While foundations create stability from which structures and relationships can emerge and grow, cornerstones help connect a structure's outline to create a solid framework. When we build a physical structure, we place cornerstones first since all other stones are set in relation to them. They determine the structure's entire position and its internal integrity. If cornerstones aren't properly anchored or placed, the structure risks coming out of alignment as it settles into its foundation. If the structure becomes skewed, it may be unable to withstand upheaval, micro shifts, or macro stresses

5. See https://www.npr.org/2017/08/20/544861933/how-one-man-convinced-200-ku-klux-klan-members-to-give-up-their-robes to watch a short interview and read a transcript about Daryl Davis. You can also watch a more in-depth documentary on Daryl Davis in the film *Accidental Courtesy: Daryl Davis, Race & America*. For an in-depth interview with Davis about his experience, listen to Episode#1419 – Daryl Davis on The Joe Rogan Experience podcast.

over time and erode slowly or crumble quickly unless strong remedial supports are put in place.

Relationships are much like structures. They require clear boundaries and strong foundations to withstand the test of time. Even when our relationships have clear boundaries and a strong foundation underpinning them, we still encounter situations that test us. Like structures, relationships aren't static. At some point, we're forced to ask ourselves, "What do we stand for? What are we made of? How is our relationship able to withstand our ever-changing environment? Are we going to make it?"

The HTI Relationship Cornerstones are powerful tools we can lean into to help us right our relationship when it seems as if our structure may be shifting out of alignment. Using them helps us be vulnerable and stay in relation with one another while remaining in integrity with our and our relationship's values. Like architectural cornerstones that are sometimes engraved with important information we can use as touchstones, the HTI Relationship Cornerstones are engraved with reminders of what we need to come back to for us to be in alignment with one another. Each of the HTI Relationship Cornerstones is an important quality or feature upon which good relationships are based. They are:

1. Communicate Heart Truth
2. Be Curious
3. Be Open to Possibilities
4. Commit to What Is

Regardless of whether our hearts are overlapping or apart, whether conflict is sporadic or rampant, we can always choose to apply the HTI Relationship Cornerstones (individually or collectively) to create space and increase the possibility of developing further intimacy. We can use the HTI Relationship Cornerstones as we engage in the STCI process, in any conversation, or on their own. Ultimately, applying them helps us keep our hearts tethered to our relationship stake while remaining in relation with one another, allowing each of us to learn more about the other and find a place of commonality. They provide us with a compass that helps guide our hearts towards True North; the path that allows us to know where we stand, where we're aligned, and where we're heading, together.

HTI Relationship Cornerstone #1 – Communicate Heart Truth

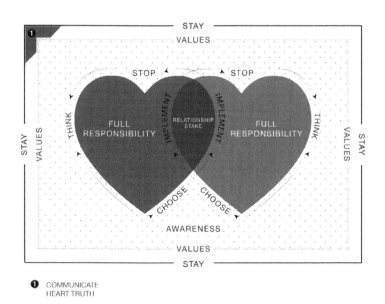

❶ COMMUNICATE
HEART TRUTH

We've all been on the receiving end of words that hurt. Whether intentional or unintentional, hurtful words can have a lasting negative impact. The adage that "sticks and stones can break your bones, but words can never hurt you" is simply untrue. Words unconsciously wielded, wielded without regard for the recipient, or wielded with malicious intent can have long-lasting impacts on the person we're in relationship with, ourself, and our relationships. Conversely, when we speak truthful words reflecting unconditional positive regard or expressing love, the person to whom we're speaking flourishes and our relationship tends to thrive. Our words have power; they are strong enough to create universes, lives, and relationships, and strong enough to destroy others.

According to Merriam-Webster, the word impeccable derives from the Latin word *impeccabilis*, a combination of the Latin prefix "in", meaning not, and the verb "peccare", meaning to sin. In other words, impeccable means being incapable of sinning. Sinning is defined as going against divine law or committing an offense against God. Impeccable means adhering to the highest standard of propriety or being flawless. Being impeccable with our words, one of author Don Miguel Ruiz's four personal agreements, means using our words flawlessly and not using them against others or ourselves. It comes across as:

- Having our words match our values so we show up as someone with integrity;
- Using words to express kindness (not negativity) towards others and ourself;
- Saying what we mean and meaning what we say;
- Speaking with the intention of having a positive impact.

Being impeccable with our words also means acting in a way that's in alignment with what's in our heart. Since actions often speak louder than words, when we act in a way that's at odds with what our hearts believe, and/or say yes with our head when our heart really believes no, we're not being impeccable with our words: our actions don't reflect our heart's truth.

Communicating impeccably means communicating our heart truth. Communicating heart truth allows us to share something about ourself (facts and feelings) and our situation while creating space for others to do the same. Because communicating heart truth doesn't include blame or judgment, it allows multiple perspectives to surface and co-exist on a level playing field. As perspectives appear, space is created, and we can explore and inquire about one another with the aim of deepening our understanding of each other. By engaging in this process, we can shift from a position of either/or to embrace one (or more) perspective that is more all-encompassing. It also allows us to achieve alignment and for a third way to emerge. To understand this relationship cornerstone, we need to grasp the difference between head truth and heart truth.

What is Head Truth?

Head truth is derived from our experience and knowledge. It can be used to deepen our understanding and expand our vision of what's possible. It's also important and powerful when used with neutral data (for example, we lost $2,000 last month or our new software does things that we did not expect) that can help us make new decisions and allow us to reach our common goals.

When used to promote our ego or as a source of armor, however, it's usually personal and involves judgment and criticism of the person we're talking to, our situation, or ideas put forth. Some examples include:

- ◆ You don't know what you're saying.
- ◆ You don't understand.

- It doesn't make sense to pursue that since it's not important or won't help us achieve our goals.
- There's no way this group can excel.
- That's a bad idea.

We typically have little to no curiosity about, connection to, or consideration for the person with whom we're speaking when we deliver our head truth with the aim of serving our ego or protecting ourself. In this instance, our perspective about our truth trumps everything, including the person with whom we're in relationship and/or our relationship. We're usually centered on ourself as we rigorously defend our point of view and our ego. And, our need to be right takes precedence over everything else since our ego is out to win at all costs, including the cost of our relationship.

Head truth regularly shows up when we engage in one-way communication, when we allow little to no room for discussion, when we assume there's a specific destination we must reach, and when we know what the outcome should be. It often appears as absolute. In these instances, we believe we have the answer to whatever problem or issue is being addressed and that we're the single owner of this truth. Because we have the only right answer, we don't allow for and can't accept additional options and ideas. We're certain there's a right and a wrong way. Our approach involves OR, not AND, and we regularly use the word *should* (for example, You should tell your boss no. You should stop cooking for your husband so he sees what he'll be missing. You should lose weight and take better care of yourself.). We're focused on getting the other person to agree with us, not on alignment, and our aim is compliance and control.

We can effectively use head truth when we want to communicate a message or make decisions in times of immediate crisis. Using it, however, often has a detrimental impact on our relationships in that it cuts off the receiver's heart, limiting their desire to get closer to us and their ability to keep their heart open and risk being vulnerable. When we speak our head truth, we often create distance between our heart and that of the person we're in relationship with. Speaking it also risks shutting down communication, tying our hands behind our backs, and, ultimately, breaking intimacy and weakening our relationships.

What is Heart Truth?

Heart truth can be diametrically opposed to head truth. It's based on our feelings and perspectives and reflects what's true for us in this moment. Articulating how we feel allows us to verbally communicate our heart's truths. "I feel happy. I feel excited. I feel frustrated. I feel mad." Feelings language, or heart truth, isn't about making accusations or assigning blame to what or who caused our feelings. Communicating our heart truth simply involves sharing how we feel.

Heart truth is flexible, malleable, creates space for exploration, and improves communication and intimacy. It's the land where feelings, perspectives, and possibilities live. Heart truth requires us to be humble, expose cracks in or lay down our armor, be open to being wrong, and, ultimately, be less than all-knowing perfection. When we express our heart truth, we're authentic, revealing, and, at times, vulnerable. Because of this exposure, it may be hard for us to access our heart truths and express them as heart thoughts.

Expressing our heart truth can take a variety of forms, including "I'm sorry and I don't know what to do next. I want to hear what you think. I want to understand what you mean. I made a mistake and I feel terrible about it." It's often recognized as such by the impact it has on bringing both its owner and the receiver alongside one another.

Sharing our heart truth allows for different perspectives to surface and for everyone to explore them within a framework of respect. Instead of "No, but…" or "Yes, but…", "Yes, and…" shows up repeatedly. "I know you're angry and frustrated, and I am too. Tell me more about what's frustrating you. I hear how you feel, and here's my perspective. How else can you express what you're feeling so I can understand your perspective."

Speaking our heart truth helps dissipate our and others' assumptions and helps us and those we're in relationship with challenge our current beliefs. Our polarities in thoughts tend to disappear as a result of expansion and exploration. We can instigate conflict and distance when we speak our head truth by glossing over important details and assuming the other person knows what we mean, intend, or hope. Conversely, speaking from our heart creates clarity and, as we gain clarity, it becomes easier to be open to whatever is emerging and avoid the unspoken stories we tell ourselves in our heads.

Olivier and I, for example, were having an ongoing and prolonged disagreement about the way he handled a situation involving our families. Each time I brought it up, he would counter by stonewalling and telling me he was too busy to talk about it in that moment. The longer this went on, the more I retreated into head truth, telling him, "We need to talk about this. You need to deal with this. You're creating a bigger problem by not dealing with the issue." My head truth–based commentary was rooted in a narrative I'd created in isolation and airing it was only exacerbating our differences.

Finally, one night, Olivier courageously accessed his heart truth and told me the reason he didn't want to talk about it. "I want the same things as you do, I just don't know what to do or how to get there and feel shame because of it." Showing his vulnerability, unease, and uncertainty immediately shifted my perception of being on opposite sides of a divide, where each of us wanted a different outcome. My heart opened and I felt myself come alongside him so we could solve the problem together. Approaching each other from this new place allowed us to examine different options and made us both more forgiving as we, together, tried different solutions with varying successes.

When we speak our heart truth, we have a greater concern for our relationship than our message or our ego. Our relationship is more important than a specific outcome, and connection is our goal. In expressing our heart truth, we often promote an atmosphere in which trust and creative generation abound, context and themes prevail over content and details, and each person feels seen and heard. Using heart-centered communication allows us to create and strengthen relationships where alignment, connection, and mutual respect are strong.

We often experience heart truth as a collaborative journey where information flows both ways, not towards a specific destination or pre-determined outcome. It can center both of us as to where we are in the present moment before we consider what's next and how we want to explore it. Heart truth is what often moves people from standing face-to-face in an adversarial manner to standing beside one another looking at the problem from the same side of the table. It's from this place that we can begin to build together.

Is Heart Truth Better than Head Truth?

Conversations, like relationships, are a dance. And, they're happening all the time at work, at home, and in the street as we go about our daily lives. They're also happening in person and through technology. Throughout these conversations, we don't always agree with people, nor do they with us. We each have our own perspectives and opinions, even while knowing they may not be viewpoints that others share.

While we can approach our lives and people we're in relationship with solely from our head, thinking our way through and acting accordingly rarely helps us create a stable foundation. In fact, operating from our heads and from a fixed mindset (i.e., one where we have everything all figured out) typically makes our lives and relationships more challenging and can make navigating differences feel overwhelming. Conversely, approaching our lives and relationships and their ongoing dynamics from our hearts helps us create a solid and stable foundation from which we can grow. Communicating our heart truth to others often invites them to do so as well.

When in relationship, we're always free to choose to use our head or heart truth, or both. Sometimes, choosing to speak head truth is our best option. For example, when Josh and I ski together and he gets too close to a cornice, I opt to use my head truth and tell him in a loud and urgent voice to stay away from the cliff's edge. While this may be the most effective choice in the moment, since my desired outcome is clear, involving no shades of gray, it works best for our relationship if I circle back later on to check in with him, explain why I spoke to him the way I did ("I was worried you'd get hurt and wanted to stop it from happening"), and make sure he has a chance to express anything that's in his heart. Failing to circle back after we express our head truth can create a situation in which the person on the receiving end of our head truth puts walls around their heart and casts judgments in their head. This typically results in relational distance, feelings of separation, and disconnection.

Communicating our heart truth also allows us to respond with authenticity and an awareness of our intention and avoid being ruled by our ego or descending into defensiveness when responding to someone who's talking to us from a place of head truth. If, for example, someone tells us we're wrong for what we believe, we can use heart truth as the basis for our response. Instead of arguing with them as to why we're right, stating our heart truth allows us to be clear on what we believe and mean to say while creating space for open discussion and exploring what else may also be true. It can be as simple as asking the other person to "tell me more," before articulating what we feel.

Given that researchers have reported that more than 70% of our communication is non-verbal, our body language, movement, stance, proximity, and posture all contribute to the quality of our relationship's communication. We can use our non-verbal body language to communicate our heart truth. Smiling as we speak or listening silently with an open facial expression may be enough. Listening with our heart as we allow space for multiple perspectives to emerge and co-exist with equal value, staying present and focused as we hear different perspectives being shared, and centering our attention on the other person and their perspectives is another form of heart truth communication. When we align our non-verbal communication with our heart truth, we're engaging in a powerful and relationship-enhancing practice.

Knowing the distinction between head truth and heart truth, and having an awareness of where we're operating from at any given moment, is foundational for navigating our relationships with grace and intention. Developing the skills to communicate from both our head and our heart gives us the ability to intentionally choose the impact we want to have, creates opportunity for exceptional collaborative experiences, and helps bring our hearts together in harmony.

Ultimately, communicating our heart truth helps us remain connected as we seek to understand one another when we, they, or both of us are not at peace. No matter whether we're communicating a truth or responding to one, communicating our heart truth helps us be and stay vulnerable which, in turn, creates intimacy, attachment, and affinity. This helps us transform our relationships into ones that are wholesome, truthful, fruitful, and interdependent. Choosing to use our creative power to manifest our heart's desires through our words and actions allows us to construct the world and relationships we want to live in.

HTI Relationship Cornerstone #2 – Be Curious

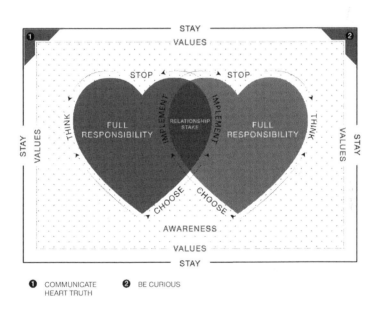

It's common for us not to know or understand another person: how they feel, what they believe, how they see the world, and how they interpret events, even when we're experiencing the world by their side. In fact, our lack of knowing and understanding is often an everyday occurrence. We may find this frustrating, especially when we're in relationship and we don't know or understand what the other person is thinking, feeling, experiencing, and intending.

It's in these times of uncertainty that we sometimes take what's said or done personally. We may become irritated and, potentially, defensive when someone says something that feels like a personal attack or criticism. Our reactions may be:

To the words said	◆ That's dumb.
To the energy with which words are said	◆ He's talking loudly so he must be mad at me.
	◆ She's so abrupt, I must have done something to offend her.
As a result of specific or layered memories and/or self-perceptions we've integrated into our lenses throughout our lifetimes	◆ When he tells me the skirt doesn't look good on me he must mean I'm fat since that's what my mom always told me.

The net effect of thinking the other person is criticizing us or doesn't understand us, our intentions, or the situation is we get triggered, defensive, or aggressive and focus on proving our innocence or rightness (That's not dumb. Stop yelling at me – I didn't do anything! How dare you call me fat!). This tends to shut down our lines of communication and often increases the level of conflict we're experiencing, effectively limiting our ability to understand each other while placing restrictions on expanding what's possible.

In this situation, we have two choices: we can get furious or we can get curious. Allowing our frustration to turn to anger and irritation often causes us to escalate our situation by blaming, labeling, criticizing, and judging the person in front of us. It can also manifest itself in the form of self-judgment, and feelings of insecurity and disappointment in ourselves. No matter how it manifests, when we get furious, we almost always create misalignment and distance between ourselves and the person we're in relationship with.

Even if our initial and common reaction to a situation is frustration, we can always make the choice to seek understanding. We can be curious about:

Ourself	◆ What am I assuming I know about them that I might be wrong about?
	◆ Where am I contributing to the confusion/conflict?
The other person	◆ What's causing them to have that viewpoint/perception?
	◆ Which of their core values are being trampled on?
Our situation	◆ What's really going on?
	◆ What has been missed?
	◆ What might we need to know to have a better understanding?

Being curious allows us to get clearer on what another person's reality is and develop a more precise picture of what's going on.

It's easier to be curious about someone when we recognize there's a good chance that what the person said has nothing to do with us. In other words, by moving out of selfishness and self-centeredness, and recognizing that we're not the center of the world nor the focus of other people's, we create freedom for ourself to reject what other people say as absolute truth. Instead, we can accept it may be truth for them and that our truth can co-exist peacefully with theirs. We don't need to go head to head in a battle to prove who's right and who's wrong. Adopting this perspective allows us to stay in relationship with someone else, regardless of whether we see things with the same lens as they do or hold the same perspective.

Being curious requires we stop thinking about what's happening or what we think should be happening and start wondering about what might be. It involves getting curious about the other person and their perspective and asking them to tell us more about what they're thinking and feeling, asking them what their thoughts and feelings are about the situation and what it means to them, and asking for more information in general about the layers that lie beneath each of their statements or beliefs. Essentially, it involves asking open-ended questions. Examples of some open-ended curiosity-based questions include:

♦ What does that mean to you?

♦ What's important about that for you?

♦ How does this make you feel?

♦ What else?

Every answer we receive provides us with much data we can use to further our conversation, gain clarity, and acquire a deeper heart-centered understanding of our situation and the person we're in relationship with.

Being curious while fully accepting the other person, regardless of their immediate views and/or behavior, and holding the other person's well-being as our highest goal creates room for us to develop compassion (sympathetic concern for someone else's sufferings or misfortunes) and empathy (the ability to understand and share someone else's feelings). By partnering with another person with the sole goal of being curious about them (their perceptions, thoughts, feelings, and truths), we gain a sense of freedom to explore unforeseen possibilities not immediately apparent.

Being curious about someone's perspective can be scary for us and for the person we're talking to. Asking questions about their point of view may come across as if we're asking for more evidence to tip the argument to our side or we may start to feel as if by exploring their perspective we're helping to tip the scales in their favor. When we come from a place of genuine curiosity, however, we're not casting judgment, stacking evidence, or building our case. Instead, we're in a place of discovery where we're simply trying to go from a place of not knowing and not understanding, a place of misalignment, to a place of deeper understanding, knowing, and possible alignment. Being curious is a heart-centered discovery into another person's perspective that allows us to journey together down pitch-black avenues and use our curiosity to begin turning lights on.

Actively listening and reflecting back what we hear being said makes it easier for us to explore the unknown together. Mirroring what the other person says back to them without applying our judgments and labels creates space for them to confirm or reformulate their positions which, in turn, helps both of us gain clarity. Using our curiosity to guide us in formulating open-ended questions we genuinely want to hear the answers to (for example, What does that mean to you? What do you hope to accomplish? What are some of your desires?) helps us achieve greater understanding by allowing different truths to simultaneously exist. Being curious helps us identify shared perspectives, commonalities, and a space in which both our hearts and minds can move towards one another, overlap, and align.

HTI Relationship Cornerstone #3 – Be Open to Possibilities

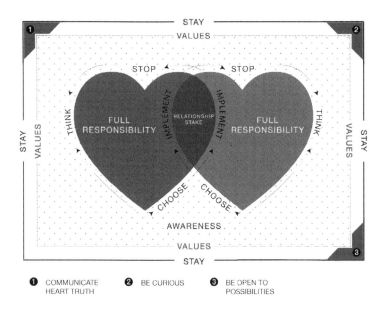

❶ COMMUNICATE HEART TRUTH　❷ BE CURIOUS　❸ BE OPEN TO POSSIBILITIES

We all make assumptions and we make them all the time. As living, breathing, assumption-making machines, we make assumptions about:

Our environment　　◆ Of course, there will be traffic on the road this evening.

Specific outcomes　　◆ Of course, the tickets to that concert will be sold out by the time I try to buy them.

Strangers' reactions to requests	♦ Of course, they're going to say no to refunding me my money for my broken chair since it's after the two-week return policy.
General scenarios	♦ I'll never find parking.
The future	♦ Of course, all cars will be self-driving and electric.

Quite often, our assumptions are negative ones.

In any given moment, however, we never really know what's coming next. While we can guess and sometimes have accurate predictions, our prediction skills aren't always spot on. The future's uncertain and, even when our best assumptions are masterfully crafted, what's coming next is often unknown. When we're in relationship, our degree of uncertainty increases since each of us processes and thinks uniquely.

As we sit in the unknown, we often try to fill the gap between knowing and not knowing by making assumptions about the person in front of us. We make assumptions about:

What the other person is thinking	♦ I know she's saying she likes the book I gave her, but I bet she doesn't since she hasn't read it.
What motivates them	♦ I know he's only taking the job because he wants the title and salary, not because he really likes the work.
What they're trying to communicate	♦ Even though she said thank you, I know she doesn't really mean it.

What they're trying to achieve and accomplish	◆ He says he wants to stay home and spend time with his family, but I know he's really waiting out the recession until he can find a higher-paying job.
The end results they're pursuing	◆ She wants to be top of her class so she can be recruited by the city's most prestigious law firm.

With each assumption we make, we lose an opportunity to communicate with the person we're in relationship with and gain insight into them and our relationship. With each missed communication, we have a greater possibility of misinterpreting events, of making wrong predictions about intent and outcomes, of hurt feelings, anger, lack of respect, and unnecessary drama. If we don't address these, they can lead to distance, which may lead to a relationship rupture that's difficult to repair as the chasm between objective reality and our perceptions becomes too wide for us to traverse. By making individual assumptions and never addressing them, we may create an unproductive and exhausting reality for ourselves that might otherwise never exist.

Being open to what's currently emerging in our environment, our hearts and minds, and in our relationship without trying to anticipate the next moment or making assumptions about it is key to being open to possibilities. Being open to what's emerging means approaching what people say, our current situation, and the future with interest, curiosity, and even desire, without imposing our expectations or being attached to specific outcomes. It involves being fully present and engaged in the process and the other person while being aware that there's a world of possibilities beyond what's immediately obvious to us. Essentially, it involves playing the game of maybe (maybe this is true, and maybe it's not; maybe this is what's next, maybe it's not).

Being open to infinite possibilities allows us to look at the same facts from different perspectives. Perspectives refers to the view or vantage point from which we're looking at our internal and external worlds. Being able to see our worlds from multiple perspectives opens the spectrum of what's possible and allows us to intentionally shape our reality and relationships.

In the film *A Few Good Men*, there's a famous courtroom scene in which Jack Nicholson is on the stand and Tom Cruise, the prosecutor, is trying to get to the truth about a past situation. After some significant posturing and maneuvering, Nicholson explodes with, "You can't handle the truth!" At some point in our lives, most of us have assumed the person in front of us can't handle the truth. Doing this allows us to speak behind their back about all the reasons we've made up about their inability to handle our feedback, feelings, or perspectives. When push comes to shove and we find ourselves face-to-face with this person, we avoid communicating our heart truth in part because we're not open to the possibility that they're resourceful enough to handle what we have to say. This common example illustrates our frequent unwillingness to be open to possibilities while making assumptions about outcomes and the abilities of people we're in relationship with.

We can avoid making assumptions and be open to what's emerging, and to new possibilities, by questioning what we know and by challenging our beliefs. Is it true what he says means what I think it means? Is it certain the outcome I think is going to happen will happen? Is it true she feels the way I think she feels? Questioning what we think we know as truth allows us to stay in the present, be open to infinite emerging possibilities, and co-create with the person and/or situation in front of us, not the fiction residing in our minds.

The easiest way for us to avoid making assumptions is by moving into action and sharing our internal heart-centered dialogue in service of our relationship. This first involves us asking an open-ended question based on "What if?" instead of stating what we think should be. The next steps involve asking "And then what's possible?" and sharing these "what ifs" openly with the person we're in relationship with. "What if I quit my job and looked at other possibilities? What if I told the truth? What if I left my spouse? What if I tried harder? What if I was more vulnerable? What if we stopped having these meetings and looked at other options? What if we charged more for our services? What if I don't show up today and looked at what else I could do? What if we can't afford our lifestyle? What if I didn't have to work? What if I won the lottery? What if we sold the company?" Starting with a question, together, we can look at possibilities without being attached to a specific outcome and judgment.

Asking questions increases our ability to understand events, another person, and available possibilities. By questioning ourselves and others, expanding our options, and looking for holes in what we believe to be true, we create space for exploring what's possible. Being open to possibilities is where magic resides. It's where we explore vulnerabilities, create intimacy, innovate, and where our hearts come closer together. Implementing this relationship cornerstone allows us to access and create infinite possibilities for ourselves and our relationships.

HTI Relationship Cornerstone #4 – Commit to What Is

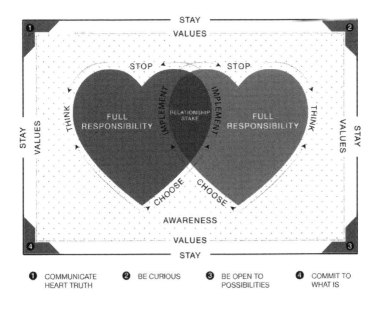

When life happens to us, for us, and, at times it seems, against us, one thing is for sure: the situation simply is. It is what it is. For us to experience anything, the event is either happening in the moment or it's already happened. And, some days are better than others. On some days, we show up as the best and most powerful version of the person we know ourself to be, fully in integrity with what we believe and value, fully present to those we love and engage with, bringing our whole selves to the table to add value and serve others based on whatever the situation requires. On other days, we fall far short of this ideal. We may fall short because we've had a lack of sleep, are hungry, aren't engaged, are upset, are distracted, are in a different head/heart space, or simply don't feel like playing all out. And, it's on the days we fall short of our ideal self that we often feel as if we haven't done our best and start to engage in negative self-talk.

We can only ever do our best with what we have available to us in the present moment. At any given moment, our level of readiness, training, skill, emotional intelligence, and overall capacity and capability varies. While we can alter our capacity and capability over the long term, we're always a collection of our current abilities. Doing our best means doing our best with wherever we are in this moment in time and with whatever resources are currently available to us. Our best looks different from day to day and hour to hour.

Showing up authentically and committing to what is means bringing our whole self to the table, whether that self is tired, cranky, angry, loving, energized, attuned to another or not, and not pretending to be something we're not. Not pretending, for example, to be happy when we're sad, agreeable when we disagree, to say we believe in something we don't just to get along, etc.

Recognizing our best is always the best we can do given what's available to us gives us freedom from self-judgment and negative self-talk, both of which tend to lead to defensiveness, righteousness, and hearts apart. Committing to what is means taking the opportunity to bring our authentic self to the table to navigate any situation that arises. It also means staying in relationship with ourself and others with the aim of honoring our deepest values and the best version of our relationship that can exist in this moment.

Committing to what is means staying with our situation or our relationship as it's currently evolving, not the situation or relationship we wish we were in. It requires acknowledging our desire for things to be different (he should do…, she shouldn't…., I wish…) while accepting what's in front of us (he is…, she isn't…, it is…, it isn't…) and working with it as it appears, not as we wish it were. When we're committed to what is, we commit to remaining in relationship no matter what shows up (for example, harmony/conflict, alignment/discord, values rubbing up against each other, behavior that's admirable, and distasteful or offensive choices) and to finding a way of moving through non-harmonious situations so our hearts move towards one another.

Committing to what is doesn't mean we need to ignore problems or accept them without having any intent of changing our situation moving forward. What staying and committing ourselves to what is does mean is accepting what is (for example, we're attracted to someone else, our mother is being abusive towards us, our co-worker is difficult to work with) without judgment (i.e., it doesn't mean anything about us and we aren't required to act based on it) as we show up authentically, transparently, and meaningfully in our relationships.

This may, for example, involve committing to our marriage while acknowledging our attraction to someone other than our spouse, acknowledging the attraction without acting on it, recommitting to our relationship with our spouse and the life we've created together, exploring the underlying reasons for why we're having these feelings, and looking for solutions to the lack of intimacy we're experiencing with our spouse. Or, it may involve staying in relation with our mother who has Alzheimer's and become abusive towards us, visiting her frequently and helping to care for her while honoring our disappearing connection and relationship even as we care for ourselves by taking space from the situation when needed. Alternatively, it may look like fully engaging with a colleague who often snaps at us and criticizes our work while working with them to create some boundaries and guidelines around working together.

When we intentionally and authentically participate in whatever emerges, we, as flawed humans, supersede the sum of our parts, both individually and as a collective. No matter how flawed we are when coming to the table, choosing to show up and engage, regardless of what emerges, means we have an awareness of ourselves as imperfect beings, an awareness of ourselves in the context of other people, and an awareness that we matter. Showing up fully makes our presence meaningful, irrespective of how much or how little we're contributing or the quality of what we're contributing to the present moment.

Intentionally choosing to participate in our relationships, actively staying in and with them, and committing to what is ensures we take responsibility for them. It doesn't mean blindly committing to our relationships no matter what emerges (for example, staying in an abusive relationship that doesn't serve us). Instead, it means by choosing to stay, we step all in regardless of what shows up, knowing we always have a choice and can create from it.

Taking responsibility empowers us to find meaning, value, and creativity in our relationships and use this as an instrument to create conditions where our hearts can come together, overlap with one another, and, ultimately, intertwine. No matter what situation we find ourselves in, committing to *what is* is a powerful relationship cornerstone that helps us establish the start line from which we can move forward, together.

Using HTI Relationship Cornerstones in Conversation

We often hear people talk about how they need to have a difficult conversation. By difficult, we generally understand the person to mean they anticipate discomfort. They're afraid that when they share information, they'll hurt the person on the receiving end. They're afraid of the conflict or relationship rupture that might ensue. They're afraid they don't have the tools to engage in the conversation. Or, they're afraid that having the conversation won't change anything and they won't achieve agreement. Using the HTI Relationship Cornerstones allows us to remove the "difficult" from conversation and work towards achieving alignment. Applying the HTI Relationship Cornerstones helps us move out of our comfort zone and into powerful and fulfilling conversations that can enrich and deepen our relationships.

Matt and I leaned into the four HTI Relationship Cornerstones when we had our final conversation to determine whether and how we would work together. It happened during a Co-Active™ Leadership retreat after we were instructed to find alignment around what we'd be doing together for our project. While we had touched on some of the issues standing in our way, there was clearly more under the surface and it wasn't obvious how we'd move forward or what we would unearth.

"Let's go sit on that bench in the sunshine," Matt said.

As we settled in, straddling the bench and looking at each other face-to-face, I wondered where to begin. Taking a deep breath, I said, "So, we've been having this conversation off and on all week and I'm getting the feeling that there's more for you under the surface. I've noticed we get to a certain point and then you run away, almost like it's too much for you."

"Yeah, well, as you know, I don't like conflict. And, I'm trying to stay and change my patterns."

"I really appreciate that you're doing that. I can see it's not easy for you and you're still committed to trying. And, I also wanted to say upfront that it hasn't been so easy for me either. I don't know why, we don't even really know each other, but you matter to me."

"Thanks. I kind of feel the same way. We really connected on our last flight home and I saw the possibilities."

"Me too. And I'm wondering… You mentioned you had reservations about working together and what it would mean for your current business. I already know you think I'm a Venus flytrap," I said laughing.

"I can't believe you're laughing about that. Do you know what a Venus flytrap is?" Matt asked incredulously.

"Of course, I do, and that's why I think it's funny. I'm curious as to why you think I might be one. Why don't you tell me a little more about what your concerns are?"

"Well, I feel like MoreCo, my current company, repre-sents so much of who I am. I was an employee for most of my working life and then I went out on my own as MoreCo. I've been having success and the success has been on my terms, which is validating because I've been living into my values. My company reflects who I am and that's emerging. I'm worried that working together would mean I'd have to give it up or I'd lose it, or even myself. I guess I'm worried I'll lose what I've created too." Matt finally exhaled and met my eyes. "Wow, it actually feels good to say all that out loud."

"Thanks for being so open with me. I can understand what you're feeling. As you know, I have my own company too. I think the difference between us is that I've been on my own for almost my whole career and while I've been successful, I'm ready to let it go for something I see as better. For a long time, though, I was like you. I wanted to see how far I could go on my own and what I could accomplish, and I guess I've proved whatever I needed to prove to myself. I now want to create with someone else. That's my priority. I can understand your fear and your reluctance to give it up. It took me a long time to get there myself. And, I want to say, I would never force you to give anything up. I just don't feel doing that would be productive, for our business or for our relationship. I also feel that if we're successful in whatever we do, there will be a natural tipping point when you might decide it's more worth it for you to be all in together than on your own, or partially in and partially out. And I think it's a process, not something we have to decide all at once, right here and now."

Matt exhaled a big sigh of relief. "Thanks for saying that. I have a bit of a box brain where I like to compartmentalize things so hearing you say I don't have to make a choice right away is super helpful. It kind of makes me more willing to continue talking about this."

As I heard the chime calling us to lunch in the distance, Matt said, "Why don't we go continue our conversation while we eat." As we ambled down the hill towards the eating hall, I noticed the atmosphere around us had become a bit lighter. Matt seemed more relaxed if not totally open, and yet I was still feeling a heaviness and tension in my chest. I was definitely not totally at ease and consciously making an effort to breathe more slowly and relax myself.

As we sat down to eat, Matt started to speak. "There's also the issue of my wife. I decided a long time ago that I'd never get divorced. I'm really protective of my marriage and I'm worried about how she might feel about me working with a woman."

Hearing this, I looked up from my plate and asked him, "Have you talked with her about this? I'm wondering because we've been talking about working together for three months now and I've raised it with my husband."

Looking flummoxed, Matt said, "No, I guess I haven't. I just assumed it would be a problem. I will talk to her. When I get home."

172 LEAD FROM YOUR HEART

"Great. I also want to say I understand about being protective of your marriage. My marriage is important to me too. It's my second marriage and I put myself on a budget after my first one so now that I've used up my only chit, I'm pretty careful about trying not to blow it. Besides, I really love my husband."

"Thanks for saying that. I guess my wife and I have experienced so many threats to our marriage that I'm reluctant to let anyone else in. Now that I understand where you're coming from, I'm actually feeling a bit more open. And, I still have a story going on that you think we're going to be friends. That you think that you and your husband and me and my wife will go out to dinner and hang out."

"Sure, it's possible. It doesn't need to happen. And I believe that it's a possibility," I said with a shrug.

"Nope. It's never going to happen." Matt stated with conviction.

"How come?"

Matt looked at me and calmly said, "I just like to keep things separate. If we work together, you can be in this box over here, where we work. But that's it. You can't touch the box that my wife and family are in. I want to keep everything separate." As I looked back at him, checking his plate to see if he let his different foods touch each other (thankfully he did), he said, "I'm going to go get some more food. I'll be back and we can talk more then."

While Matt was gone, I thought about what he'd said and realized that having those kinds of limitations put on me from the outset was never going to work for me. As he sat back down in front of me, I said, "I understand you like to keep things separate but I don't want to be put in a box and I can't move forward with you if those are going to be the parameters."

"Well, ok. Maybe a box is too extreme. It's more like my life is a pie and you're in this wedge and my family is in this one next to it. You can touch up against them, but they're still separate. I definitely see you in my life. And ok, maybe if we were to run into each other on the ski hill in Whistler, we'd ski a run or two together. You are part of the whole pie."

My head was swimming with this new information, and I noticed I had become even more tense as Matt had relaxed into his explanation. I realized going down this path wasn't going to help us get off it or move us forward, so I asked, "Why don't we just focus on now and worry about how things will unfold later? What can we agree on now?"

"What a great idea. I'm back in my box brain. I'll talk with my wife about us working together when I get home and, for now, let's just decide how we're going to work together and what we can agree on. I'm going to write it down or I'll forget it."

"Great! I know you're important to me and this relationship is too. And I think you feel the same way."

"Agreed. And, I see a lot of possibilities. And I want to do this initial project with you. 100%."

In the end, what we wrote down was, "We're in alignment that we matter to each other. This relationship is important, and we're open to exploring the possibilities, beginning with our project."

When we were done, I realized I felt as if a big weight was taken off my chest and said, "Wow, that was intense."

"Really? You found that intense? I didn't find that so intense."

"I know. I'm usually great with intensity and I found our conversation super intense. I wonder why?"

"I guess you found it more intense than I did because you didn't know if I was going to run again whereas I knew I'd finally decided to stop running and stay and work it out with you."

By staying, exploring each other's values, feelings, and perspectives, by having an awareness of what was shifting in our environment, and by engaging in STCI as we leaned into the four HTI Relationship Cornerstones, we were able to work through our conflict and come out in relationship, stronger, with our hearts together. As we've gotten to know each other better, we've become more competent at engaging in this type of conversation and it's become a way of being that's provided both of us with enriching growth and creativity. Conversations are no longer difficult or prefaced with an adjective. They simply are.

Working the HTI Relationship Cornerstones

Being in relationships takes work. Navigating the associated pleasures and pains we encounter combined with external influences can place pressure on our relationships. The HTI Relationship Cornerstones are tried, tested, and true and are integral for building exceptionally strong, fruitful, and rich relationships. Although they're designed to serve our relationships and are always available for us to use, we sometimes get in our own way and are unable to lean into them because our ego, emotional weapons and shields, and reptilian brain of fight or flight prevents us from accessing them. As we try to shoulder situations and circumstances on our own, we can find ourselves blinded by emotion and alone.

Leaning into the HTI Relationship Cornerstones and using them to navigate our circumstances and conversations can help us create healthy relationships in which our hearts and minds are aligned. Communicating our heart truth, being curious, being open to possibilities, and committing to what is, regardless of how difficult or easy the moment or how much or how little we have to contribute, all help us create the conditions in which creativity can emerge and our relationships can expand. Making use of the HTI Relationship Cornerstones requires us to:

- Be willing to let go of "knowing" the truth and accepting that multiple truths are possible;
- Let go of or suspend our beliefs for a moment;
- Have a true heartfelt desire to understand another person's perspective;
- Be humble, release our ego, and look to grab hold of what's possible in partnership;
- Allow things to unfold and explore new paths and ideas we've never previously considered;
- Agree to temporarily do things we disagree with to explore "what if";
- Breathe, relax, and try some new perspectives and options on for size;
- Stop thinking win/lose and right/wrong and begin activating our curiosity and expansiveness;
- Suspend our belief that a decision needs to be made right away and that it's final;
- Suspend the belief that perspectives are permanent solutions;
- Remember that change is inevitable, valuable, and an opportunity for growth.

Ultimately, if we do this, we can easily access the HTI Relationship Cornerstones to remove the difficult from our conversations, keep our relationships in harmonious alignment as we grow towards our desired state, and move, together, through conflict along the way.

Key Points

♦ The four HTI Relationship Cornerstones create a stable foundation and solid framework from which we can lean into, respond to, and create from any condition and circumstance we experience in our relationships – individually or together.

♦ The cornerstone *Communicate Heart Truth* creates space for exploration; it requires us to be authentic, humble, vulnerable, and express how we feel.

♦ The cornerstone *Be Curious* is served when we authentically ask open-ended questions and seek to learn and understand more about someone's perspective.

♦ The cornerstone *Be Open to Possibilities* involves being open to what's currently emerging in our environment, our hearts and minds, and in our relationship without trying to anticipate or make assumptions about the next moment.

♦ The cornerstone *Commit to What Is* supports us in acknowledging the truth and committing to what is, without judgment, helping us establish the start line from which we can move forward, together.

♦ Applying the HTI Relationship Cornerstones allows us to engage in powerful and fulfilling conversations that can enrich and deepen our relationships.

Putting Concepts into Practice

Practice #1

Re-read Tanya and Matt's conversation in the *Using HTI Relationship Cornerstones in Conversation* section of this chapter. As you read, identify where you see each of the four HTI Relationship Cornerstones and/or label where each cornerstone is being modeled in the conversation.

Practice #2

Write down the four HTI Relationship Cornerstones. Reflect on and journal the following questions:

- Which cornerstone(s) comes most naturally to you? How does this show up in your life and relationships?
- Which cornerstone(s) do you find most difficult to lean into? How does this difficulty show up in your life and relationships?

Practice #3

Discuss the four HTI Relationship Cornerstones with your partner, family member(s), team, etc. Use the following questions to stimulate an open discussion and allow each person to answer:

- What do the HTI Relationship Cornerstones mean to you? Note: There is no right or wrong response here.
- What is the HTI Relationship Cornerstone you're most comfortable using and why? Which one is most uncomfortable for you to consider using and why?

- What are the benefits of using these in our relationship? In our team? What are the costs of using them?
- What are three to five examples of how we could bring each relationship cornerstone to life?

We always have a choice. We can stay in a reactive state or choose to take full responsibility for ourselves and our relationships. Which choice will create the world you want to live in?

.

CHAPTER EIGHT

So, What Now?

Most of us have had experiences in our lives that immediately provoke the expression "WTF?" or "What The F*#!?" Typically, this response is triggered when we perceive something is wrong or isn't going as planned. Our WTF reactions are natural, important, and a sign that we care passionately about whatever is unfolding. We're invested, and our hearts and minds are committed. Expressing WTF helps us communicate our feelings, provides an outlet for our emotion, and releases energy. It establishes an exclamation mark for the narrative we're giving to our current experience.

Unfortunately, reacting with WTF doesn't improve our situation. It doesn't help us address whatever caused our reaction – or resolve it. For many people, relationships, teams, and organizations, WTF can set the stage for blame, excuses, and finger-pointing. WTF becomes a roadblock, an obstacle, and a time and resource waster. It stops us from working through conflict and reaching our desired outcomes, together.

From WTF to SWN (So What Now)

When I was growing up, the following quote was taped to my parents' fridge, "Relax, nothing is under control." Well, like most kids, I didn't listen to everything that my parents told me and instead set out to reach my dreams with a well laid out set of plans I believed I would have full control over. Unfortunately, as I started putting my plans into action, I began encountering setbacks.

Some were small, like discovering my dream job wasn't so dreamy, or my new boss was incompetent. Some threatened my ego, like learning my dazzling new sales strategy was replicated (only better) by our competitor – days before we launched. And some setbacks shook my world more profoundly, like finding out our family wasn't immune to the words, "You have cancer."

Having expectations and believing I was in control meant I found the experience of setbacks and curve balls surprising, frustrating, and sometimes debilitating. I didn't like failing and I soon began expressing myself with language I was taught not to use: WTF! What the F*#!?

Releasing steam in this way always felt good, even though the situation I was fuming about remained afterward. For me, blame was my typical next step. I'd look outside myself and cast judgment on what had just happened without taking any responsibility. My ability to follow WTF moments with an assignment of blame, backed with a well-crafted excuse or dose of victimhood, became a powerful pattern that served me well in the short term. It also limited my potential, stunted my growth, and distanced me from reality and the people around me. I masked my WTF feelings with sarcasm, becoming very adept at distracting and deflecting. What I didn't realize I was doing by sweeping things under the carpet with WTF, however, was damaging my relationships and limiting my ability to create outcomes I truly desired.

There will be countless moments in our lives where we start out with great intentions only to be thrown off course by variables and circumstances out of our control. A universally accepted, but ultimately unproductive, response is WTF! If we don't recover quickly from WTF, it can easily shift from its original, emotional, meaning to blame: Who to Fault? Where's the Fault? Why the Fault? When the Fault? While it's tempting to stay in the WTF space, focusing on it anchors us in the past, stuck on something we can no longer change. If what we want is to influence our current situation or experience and create a different outcome, we must leave WTF behind. It's time for SWN.

Great relationships and great leadership require that when problems emerge, we ask ourselves the simple question, "So, what now?" and move forward from there. While it's a simple question, it's not always easy for us to ask or answer. Doing so requires that we relinquish our desire to cast blame and accept that the past is the past. We must *Commit to What Is.* Whatever has happened has already happened and can't be changed. We must take responsibility for our current situation, look at the part we played in creating it, look for opportunities to learn from it and create a different outcome.

Choosing to stay in our relationship, in our situation, and in alignment with our values allows us to explore the SWN questions: So, what now? So, what's needed? So, what's next? So, where now? So, who now? Underlying this is the idea that all we have is now. Focusing on now keeps us present to what's happening around and within us, and to whatever is emerging. We become less reactive and more creative.

A SWN mindset is key to using the HTI Relationship Map. The STCI process and the four HTI Relationship

Cornerstones provide us with the opportunity to continually ask SWN? It's only in this moment that we have influence and can effect change. As we try on different solutions and evaluate their effectiveness, we can create from now, all the while improving our relationships and outcomes, together.

So, What's Next?

Change is constant and inescapable. We are currently undergoing change at a more rapid pace than we've ever experienced, and its pace is accelerating every day.

♦ *Technology currently impacts every area of our day-to-day lives and technological change is progressing at an unprecedented speed.* These changes impact the way we do things and how we relate to one another. Technology provides us with the means to stay in communication with one another without expending much relational or emotional energy. It can potentially create a divide that can cause our hearts to move apart, limiting our personal and leadership impact. Our ability to understand one another, create from each other, and innovate together is at risk.

♦ *We're at the mercy of climate change,* which is having an environmental, geographical, relational, political, and societal impact on all of us, not just those of us directly experiencing a change in our immediate weather or environmental habitat. Fires are lasting longer and are becoming larger and more frequent in occurrence. Flooding and other extreme weather patterns are increasing in intensity and becoming more commonplace, extending to areas previously immune to them. Climate refugees are having an impact, both on the nations they leave and the nations and societies they aspire to join. Our food supplies are being impacted in terms of quantity, quality, and availability. All of this impacts how we, as individuals and as groups, are relating and interacting with one another, limiting our ability to care for and create together.

♦ *Our cultures are also changing.* Many nations are feeling challenged with the entrance and rise of new cultural and racial groups. While this change in racial composition provides us with an opportunity for dialogue, it's also resulted in a rise in racism (for example, rise in anti-Semitism, anti-immigrant sentiment, anti-refugeeism, etc.), a polarization among economic groups, and a high level of violence in everyday life (for example, stabbings, mass shootings, suicide bombings, violence targeting women, etc.). Instead of building bridges towards one another, all these factors enhance and build on divides that further distance us from one another.

♦ *Identity politics are on the rise.* The rise of identity politics has exacerbated divides, polarizing us into artificially created opposing camps, often spilling over from the public sphere into the workplace, our personal relationships, and our homes. This limits our ability to be in relationship with one another, find commonalities, and work together towards achieving alternative outcomes that can benefit us all. What we need is leadership that recognizes the fundamental truth that we are all interconnected and interdependent so we can work together and create positive change for us all.

The question we want to leave you with is, "So, What's Next?" The answer is up to you. It's up to each of us. Each of us has the choice to stay in a reactive state or decide to take responsibility for ourselves and our relationships. We have the opportunity to create the world we want to live in and navigate our relationships together. Our ability to survive and thrive depends on our ability to stay in connection and create with and from one another. We have a choice to stay through any conflict that emerges, learn the fundamental truth of one another, and better understand each other. Making this choice allows us to capitalize on each of our strengths, compensate for our weaknesses, and hold each other up when we stumble.

Together we are better. Together we are more powerful. Together we can innovate and create. We can transform the world we're living in to one in which hearts together inspire and one that reflects what we desire. Leadership works best when it's powered by healthy relationships. The choice to engage is always ours. And, because you matter, I matter, and we matter, and we matter now, we hope your answer will involve choosing to bring hearts together to inspire what's next.

Key Points

- Our reflexes and reactions are natural, important, and a sign we care passionately.
- Staying in a WTF pattern sets the stage for blame, excuses, and finger-pointing, keeping us from working through conflict and reaching our desired outcomes, together.
- Being aware of our WTF (What the F*#!) feelings and choosing a relationship-based response of SWN (So, What Now?) is an empowering choice.
- Choosing SWN requires that we accept we cannot control or change the past and instead take full responsibility for ourself and our relationships so we can create the world we want to live in.

Putting Concepts into Practice

Practice #1

Take this book to heart. After reading it, work it! Go back to each chapter and implement each concept. It works simply, when you work it, together.

Practice #2

Share this book with people you're in a relationship with and discuss.

Practice #3

Visit HTI Institute's resource page (htiinstitute.com/resources). Download and use the tools that will bring your hearts together and improve your relationship-based leadership.

Practice #4

Engage with HTI Institute (Facebook, Instagram, LinkedIn, Podcasts, visit our website at www.htiinstitute.com).

Practice #5

Collaborate with us. Visit our website and **contact us for a conversation about how to implement relationship-based leadership.**

Practice #6

Print the HTI Relationship Map from www.htiinstitute.com/ resources. Frame it. Laminate it. Enlarge it. Make it visible. Use it to navigate and enrich your relationships.

Practice #7

Decide that relationship-based leadership matters. Enrol you and your team into an HTI Leadership Academy and be responsible for an inspiring transformation.

Recommended Further Reading

Arbinger Institute, *Leadership and Self-Deception,* is about how we can own our motivations and take full responsibility for our impact to achieve better relationships and results.

Arbinger Institute, *The Anatomy of Peace,* provides tools for moving out of conflict and into peace to better transform our relationships and outcomes.

Arbinger Institute, *The Outward Mindset,* looks at how individuals and organizations can choose their perspective and own their choices to work collaboratively through conflict to be innovative and have a positive impact.

Carol Adrienne, *Find Your Purpose, Change Your Life: Getting to the Heart of Your Life's Mission,* is a practical guide and workbook to helping you identify your life purpose.

Sue Bender, *Stretching Lessons: The Daring That Starts from Within,* is a personal exploration of how we can open ourselves, take risks, and stretch ourselves as told through topically based vignettes.

Tara Bennett-Goleman, *Emotional Alchemy,* explains mindfulness practices and consciousness and looks at how they can be used to be present, commit to what is, and build the capacity to be vulnerable and empathetic.

Brené Brown, *I Thought It Was Just Me (But It Isn't)*, looks at the role that shame plays in our decisions and our lives and how we can choose to step into our authenticity and vulnerability to own our stories and create lives and relationships that are more heartfelt.

Brené Brown, *The Gifts of Imperfection: Let Go of Who You Think You're Supposed to Be and Embrace Who You Are,* provides tools for living authentically so that we can accept ourselves and take responsibility for our choices and our relationships while bringing our entire being to the table, flaws and all.

Brené Brown, *Daring Greatly*, investigates vulnerability and how we can explore and express it in our lives and relationships to create more fruitful and generative ones.

Brené Brown, *Rising Strong*, examines how we can stay vulnerable through our conflicts and failures, own our stories, and use them to develop our resilience and grow stronger, together.

Brené Brown, *Braving the Wilderness,* focuses on how we can belong and stay in relationship with others while staying authentic and vulnerable and remaining true to ourselves and our values without sacrificing who we are and what we value.

Brené Brown, *Dare to Lead,* explores how to become a leader who is courageous, authentic, vulnerable, and who operates in alignment with their values.

Kevin Cashman, *Leadership from the Inside Out: Becoming a Leader for Life,* explores the relationship between personal responsibility and our ability to lead others and provides tools for us to develop our personal mastery.

Jim Clemmer, *Growing the Distance: Timeless Principles for Personal, Career, and Family Success,* looks at how personal choice, personal responsibility, authenticity, passion, and commitment impact our ability to grow, develop, and mobilize and engage others as we navigate change.

Richard J. Davidson and Sharon Begley, *The Emotional Life of Your Brain: How Its Unique Patterns Affect the Way You Think, Feel, and Live – and How You Can Change Them,* explains the six emotional styles and how they can influence our relationships and outcomes.

Wayne Dyer, *Inspiration: Your Ultimate Calling,* looks at what it means to be inspiring and how we can be inspiring to others.

Viktor E. Frankl, *Man's Search for Meaning,* provides a great exploration of how we can find meaning and choose to create our own perspective, regardless of the situations we find ourselves in.

Marshall Goldsmith, *What Got You Here Won't Get You There,* delves into practical actions that we can take to successfully navigate change and enhance our relationships and leadership.

Daniel Goleman, *Working with Emotional Intelligence,* explores the set of skills that influence our relationships and outcomes as well as how we can develop them.

John Gottman, *The Seven Principles for Making Marriage Work,* explains and explores seven principles identified through research that allow us to resolve conflicts, find alignment, and achieve greater levels of intimacy to create harmonious and long-lasting relationships.

Jean Houston, *A Passion for the Possible,* provides some practical exercises and raises interesting questions to explore to identify our true potential.

Joseph Jaworski, *Synchronicity: The Inner Path of Leadership*, explores how when we are present and committed to what is it becomes easier to identify possibilities and create new outcomes that were previously invisible to us.

Barry Neil Kaufman, *Happiness is a Choice*, examines how happiness is a choice that we can choose to transform any and all of our relationships.

Karen and Henry Kimsey-House, *Co-Active Leadership: Five Ways to Lead*, explains the co-active leadership model, its five dimensions, and how we can apply them to create stronger and better outcomes.

Harriet Lerner, *The Dance of Deception: A Guide to Authenticity and Truth-Telling in Women's Relationships*, looks at how we can be authentic and truthful in our interactions to create heart-centered relationships.

Harriet Lerner, *The Dance of Connection*, examines how we can use our voice, express our vulnerability, and work through conflict and to create connection in a heart-centered way.

Harriet Lerner, *The Dance of Anger: A Woman's Guide to Changing the Patterns of Intimate Relationships*, examines how we can listen to our anger and use it as a source of truth and creativity to transform our relationships.

Dave Logan, John King & Halee Fischer-Wright, *Tribal Leadership: Leveraging Natural Groups to Build a Thriving Organization*, examines the role that values play in bringing people together and helping them to successfully navigate change to create superior outcomes and results.

Mark Manson, *The Subtle Art of Not Giving a [bleep]: A Counterintuitive Approach to Living a Good Life*, examines

RECOMMENDED FURTHER READING 193

how we can take full responsibility for ourselves and how we can choose our perspectives to create our realities.

L. David Marquet, *Turn the Ship Around: A True Story of Turning Followers into Leaders,* explores how empowering others can create stronger relationships, lasting change, and improved results.

Lynne McTaggart, *The Intention Experiment,* is a review of scientific experiments that explore how our thoughts impact our reality and how we can harness them to evoke transformation.

Daniel H. Pink, *A Whole New Mind,* explores practices that we can engage in to become more creative and open, so that we can begin to identify new possibilities.

Daniel H. Pink, *Drive: The Surprising Truth About What Motivates Us,* investigates what provides us with internal motivation and how we can use this to change how we are thinking.

Dan Pontefract, *The Purpose Effect: Building Meaning in Yourself, Your Role and Your Organization,* looks at how organizations who center on purpose and values benefit every stakeholder, from employees to society in general.

Dan Pontefract, *Open to Think: Slow Down, Think Creatively and Make Better Decisions,* examines how slowing down our thinking creates a world with better outcomes.

Marcia Reynolds, *The Discomfort Zone: How Leaders Turn Difficult Conversations into Breakthroughs,* explores how we can become open to possibilities before and when in conversation.

Marshall B. Rosenberg, *Nonviolent Communication: A Language of Compassion,* provides tools for communicating in a non-violent way that allows us to move through conflict and gain a greater understanding of our situation and each other, ultimately bringing our hearts closer together.

Don Miguel Ruiz, *The Four Agreements: A Practical Guide to Personal Freedom*, provides a description and exploration of four personal agreements that we can adopt to achieve personal freedom.

Don Miguel Ruiz and Janet Mills, *The Fifth Agreement,* explores how to tap into our curiosity and be open to possibilities.

Edgar H. Schein, *Humble Inquiry: The Gentle Art of Asking Instead of Telling,* provides practical instructions on how to be curious and ask curiosity-based questions while being open to possibilities.

Susan Scott, *Fierce Conversations,* explores how to communicate effectively and have powerful conversations while staying in relationship with one another.

Martin E. P. Seligman, *Learned Optimism: How to Change Your Mind and Your Life*, looks at the interplay between our minds and bodies and explores how we can change our mindset from a pessimistic one to an optimistic one to create better relationships and outcomes in all realms of our lives.

Peter Senge, C. Otto Scharmer, Joseph Jaworski, and Betty Sue Flowers, *Presence: Human Purpose and the Field of the Future,* explores how by becoming present and committing to what is we are better able to navigate change and come out in a better place, together.

Robin Sharma, *The Monk Who Sold His Ferrari: A Spiritual Fable About Fulfilling Your Dreams and Reaching Your Destiny,* is a fable about how good relationships and integrity are central to being an effective leader.

Robin Sharma, *Leadership Wisdom from the Monk Who Sold His Ferrari: The 8 Rituals of Visionary Leaders,* is a fable about leadership and the role that self mastery and purpose play in it.

Steven J. Stein and Howard E. Book, *The EQ Edge: Emotional Intelligence and Your Success,* explains the Emotional Quotient Inventory (EQ-i) and provides an in-depth explanation of each dimension.

Michael Bungay Stanier, *The Advice Trap: Be Humble, Stay Curious & Change the Way You Lead Forever,* looks at how to tap into curiosity to gain deeper insight into another person, speak and listen to heart truth, and explore possibilities, together.

Deborah Tannen, *That's Not What I Meant! How Conversational Style Makes or Breaks Relationships,* examines the impact different conversational styles have on relationships and outcomes.

Chris Voss, *Never Split the Difference: Negotiating as If Your Life Depends on It,* shows how life is a series of negotiations requiring positive relationships for successful outcomes to result.

Margaret J. Wheatley, *Leadership and the New Science: Discovering Order in a Chaotic World,* explores the role of conflict and chaos and how our navigating it through cooperation and connection brings us to a new place.

Jocko Willink and Leif Babin, *Extreme Ownership,* explores the concept of what it means to take full responsibility for every situation and relationship that we find ourselves in.

Acknowledgements

We'd like to send a huge wave of gratitude towards Jen Moss for providing us with feedback and insights while helping us fine-tune our story, Stephanie Colegrove for pointing us towards clarity and conciseness, and Trina Hamilton for helping us bring the heart of the matter to the forefront in our storytelling and explanations.

We'd also like to thank Jennifer Papineau for bringing our Map to life in beautiful graphics that are both engaging and easy to understand, Sean Strong and Howard VanEs for creating our book cover, Greg Ioannou our editor for bringing our manuscript to a shine, Amanda Feeney for proofing it, and Meghan Behse for her gorgeous layout and guidance.

Thank you to the Co-Active Training Institute without whom we never would have blazed the path for relationship-based leadership and the Praying Mantis tribe for their ongoing support, feedback, and ever-present encouragement and cheerleading.

Tanya

I'd like to give a huge shout out to Olivier. Thank you for encouraging and supporting me throughout this process, for your unflagging belief in me as I spent day after day writing and editing this book on the couch instead of spending time with you, and for allowing me to borrow you for the stories we've included in this book. Finally, thank you to both you and Josh for showing up again and again and staying in relationship with me regardless of what shows up.

Matt, thank you for your ongoing cheerleading and participation in this project. Creating this book in partnership has been more fun, more creatively engaging, and resulted in a much better outcome than I ever could have done alone. Finally, thank you to all of my friends, clients, and family, all of whom have taught me much about relationships and leadership.

Matt

I would like to thank my wife, Susie, for believing in me and helping us create the time and space required for this undertaking. To Mike Trotman for inspiring me to "dream big" and for the many hours we have spent over the years discussing relationship-based leadership both in concept and in action. To all my clients, employers, peers, and mentors who have helped influence and contribute to the depth of this model and the impact it has. And finally, to Tanya, my business partner, for her tireless effort, drive and skills, and for contributing more than her fair share to move this book from an idea into reality.

About the Authors

Tanya Schecter and Matthew Gould are the co-founders of the HTI Institute, which specializes in relationship-based leadership. They are both passionate about improving relationships, one relationship at a time, to create a culture of leadership and excellence.

Tanya has 25+ years of experience developing curriculums and working as a trainer, coach, and performance and leadership consultant in a wide variety of industries in the public and private sectors. Tanya holds two Master's degrees from McGill University and Concordia University, is trained as a Co-Active coach, and is certified in EQ-I (emotional intelligence), Myers-Briggs, and ProSci (change management).

Matt has 25+ years of extensive experience leading teams across small, medium, and corporate businesses to increase personal leadership and effectiveness and exceed business and corporate objectives. Matthew has an undergraduate degree from UBC, is an MBS graduate from the Rotman's School of Business and is a certified professional co-active coach (CPCC).

Tanya and Matt live in Vancouver's Lower Mainland with their families, enjoy spending time outdoors, and have a passion for Grover, the most relationship-based Muppet ever.

Manufactured by Amazon.ca
Bolton, ON